Acoustic & Digital

PIANO BUYER®

MODEL & PRICE SUPPLEMENT

Spring 2020

LARRY FINE
Editor

WWW.PIANOBUYER.COM

Piano Buyer Model & Price Supplement is published by:

Brookside Press LLC
P.O. Box 601041
San Diego, CA 92160 USA

619.738.4155
619.810.0425 (fax)
info@pianobuyer.com
www.pianobuyer.com

ISBN 978-1-92914572-0

Distributed to the book trade by Independent Publishers Group,
814 North Franklin St., Chicago, IL 60610
(800) 888-4741 or (312) 337-0747
www.ipgbook.com

Reasonable efforts have been made to secure accurate information for this publication. Due in part to the fact that manufacturers and distributors will not always willingly make this information available, however, some indirect sources have been relied on.

Neither the editors nor publisher make any guarantees with respect to the accuracy of the information contained herein, and will not be liable for damages—incidental, consequential, or otherwise—resulting from the use of the information.

CONTENTS

Acoustic Piano
Model & Pricing Guide

This guide contains price information for nearly every brand, model, style, and finish of new piano that has regular distribution in the United States and, for the most part, Canada. Omitted are some marginal, local, or "stencil" brands (brands sold only by a single dealership). Prices are in U.S. dollars and are subject to change. Prices include an allowance for the approximate cost of freight from the U.S. warehouse to the dealer, and for a minimal amount of make-ready by the dealer. The prices cited in this edition were compiled in February 2020 and apply only to piano sales in the U.S. Prices in Canada are often very different due to differences in duty, freight, sales practices, and competition.

Note that the prices of European pianos vary with the value of the dollar against the euro. For this edition, the exchange rate used by most manufacturers was approximately €1 = $1.10. Prices of European pianos include import duties and estimated costs of airfreight (where applicable) to the dealer. However, actual costs will vary depending on the shipping method used, the port of entry, and other variables. Also keep in mind that the dealer may have purchased the piano at an exchange rate different from the current one.

Unless otherwise indicated, cabinet styles are assumed to be traditional in nature, with minimal embellishment and straight legs. Recognizable furniture styles are noted, and the manufacturer's own trademarked style name is used when an appropriate generic name could not be determined. Please see the section on "Furniture Style and Finish" in our online article "**Piano-Buying Basics**" for descriptions or definitions of terms relating to style and finish.

"Size" refers to the height of a vertical or the length of a grand. These are the only dimensions that vary significantly and relate to the quality of the instrument. The height of a vertical piano is measured from the floor to the top of the piano. The length of a grand piano is measured from the very front (keyboard end) to the very back (tail end) with the lid closed.

About Prices

The subject of piano pricing is difficult, complicated, and controversial. One of the major problems is that piano dealers tend to prefer that list prices be as high as possible so they can still make a profit while appearing to give very generous discounts. Honesty about pricing is resisted.

But even knowing what is "honest" is a slippery business because many factors can have a dramatic effect on piano pricing. For one thing, different dealerships can pay very different wholesale prices for the same merchandise, depending on:

- the size of the dealership and how many pianos it agrees to purchase at one time or over a period of time
- whether the dealer pays cash or finances the purchase
- the degree to which the dealer buys manufacturer overstocks at bargain prices
- any special terms the dealership negotiates with the manufacturer or distributor
- the cost of freight to the dealer's location.

In addition to these variations at the wholesale level, retail conditions also vary from dealer to dealer or from one geographic area to another, including:

- the general cost of doing business in the dealer's area
- the level of pre- and post-sale service the dealer provides
- the level of professionalism of the sales staff and the degree to which they are trained and compensated
- the ease of local comparison shopping by the consumer for a particular type of piano or at a particular price level.

Besides the variations between dealerships, the circumstances of each sale at any particular dealership can vary tremendously due to such things as:

- how long a particular piano has been sitting around unsold, racking up finance charges for the dealer
- the dealer's financial condition and need for cash at the moment
- competing sales events going on at other dealerships in the area
- whether or not the customer is trading in a used piano.

As difficult as it might be to come up with accurate price information, confusion and ignorance about pricing for such a high-ticket item is intolerable to the consumer, and can cause decision-making paralysis. I strongly believe that a reasonable amount of price information actually greases the wheels of commerce by giving the customer the peace of mind that allows him or her to make a purchase. In this guide I've tried to give a level of information about price that reasonably respects the interests of both buyer and seller, given the range of prices that can exist for any particular model.

Prices include a bench except where noted. (Even where a price doesn't include a bench, the dealer will almost always provide one and quote a price that includes it.) Most dealers will also include delivery and one or two tunings in the home, but these are optional and a matter of agreement between you and the dealer. Prices do not include sales tax.

In this guide, two prices are given for each model: Manufacturer's Suggested Retail Price (MSRP) and Suggested Maximum Price (SMP).

Manufacturer's Suggested Retail Price (MSRP)
The MSRP is a price provided by the manufacturer or distributor and designed as a starting point from which dealers are expected to discount. I include it here for

reference purposes—only rarely does a customer pay this price. The MSRP is usually figured as a multiple of the wholesale price, but the specific multiple used differs from company to company. **For that reason, it's fruitless to compare prices of different brands by comparing discounts from the MSRP.** To see why, consider the following scenario:

Manufacturer A sells brand A through its dealer A. The wholesale price to the dealer is $1,000, but for the purpose of setting the MSRP, the manufacturer doubles the wholesale price and sets the MSRP at $2,000. Dealer A offers a 25 percent discount off the MSRP, for a "street price" of $1,500.

Manufacturer B sells brand B through its dealer B. The wholesale price to the dealer is also $1,000, but manufacturer B triples the wholesale price and sets the MSRP at $3,000. Dealer B offers a generous 50 percent discount, for a street price of, again, $1,500.

Although the street price is the same for both pianos, a customer shopping at both stores and knowing nothing about the wholesale price or how the MSRPs are computed, is likely to come away with the impression that brand B, with a discount of 50 percent off $3,000, is a more "valuable" piano and a better deal than brand A, with a discount of 25 percent off $2,000. Other factors aside, which dealer do you think will get the sale? It's important to note that there is nothing about brand B that makes it deserving of a higher MSRP than brand A—how to compute the MSRP is essentially a marketing decision on the part of the manufacturer.

Because of the deceptive manner in which MSRPs are so often used, some manufacturers no longer provide them. In those cases, I've left the MSRP column blank.

Suggested Maximum Price (SMP)

The Suggested Maximum Price (SMP) is a price I've created, based on a profit margin that I've uniformly applied to published wholesale prices. (Where the published wholesale price is unavailable, or is believed to be bogus, which is sometimes the case, I've made a reasonable attempt to estimate the SMP from other sources.) Because in the SMP, unlike in the MSRP, the same profit margin is applied to all brands, the SMP can be used as a "benchmark" price for the purpose of comparing brands and offers. The specific profit margin I've chosen for the SMP is one that dealers often try—but rarely manage—to attain. Also included in the SMP, in most cases, are allowances for duty (where applicable), freight charges, and a minimal amount of make-ready by the dealer. Although the SMP is my creation, it's a reasonable estimate of the **maximum** price you should realistically expect to pay. However, **most sales actually take place at a discount to the SMP**, as discussed below.

Actual Selling or "Street" Price

As you should know by now from reading this publication, most dealers of new pianos are willing—and expect—to negotiate. Only a handful of dealers have non-negotiable prices. For more information on negotiating, please see "**Negotiating Price and Trade-Ins**" in our online article "Piano Buying Basics." *The Piano Book* also gives advice about negotiating tactics.

How good a deal you can negotiate will vary, depending on the many factors listed earlier. But in order to make a budget, or to know which pianos are within your budget, or just to feel comfortable enough to actually make a purchase, you need some idea of what is considered normal in the industry. In most cases, discounts from the Suggested Maximum Price range from 15 to 25 percent. This does *not* mean that if you try hard enough, you can talk the salesperson into giving you a 25 percent discount. Rather, it reflects the wide range of prices possible in the marketplace due to the many factors discussed earlier. For budgeting purposes only, I suggest figuring a discount of about 20 percent. This will probably bring you within about 5 percent, one way or the other, of the final negotiated price. Important exception: Discounts on Steinway pianos generally range from 0 to 10 percent. For your convenience in figuring the effects of various discounts, a discount calculator is included in the model and price database, accessible through our website.

There is no single "fair" or "right" price that can be applied to every purchase. The only fair price is that which the buyer and seller agree on. It's understandable that you would like to pay as little as possible, but remember that piano shopping is not just about chasing the lowest price. Be sure you are getting the instrument that best suits your needs and preferences, and that the dealer is committed to providing the appropriate level of pre- and post-sale service.

Searchable Database

To search piano models by price range, size, quality level, furniture style, finish, and more, please go to **www.pianobuyer.com** to access the free searchable database of acoustic piano models and prices.

Model	Feet	Inches	Description	MSRP	SMP
BALDWIN					
Verticals					
B342		43	French Provincial Satin Cherry	10,865	7,790
B442		43	Satin Mahogany	10,865	7,790
BP1		47	Polished Ebony	9,595	6,990
BP1/S		47	Polished Ebony with Silver Hardware	9,895	7,190
B243		47	Satin Ebony/Walnut (school piano)	10,865	7,790
BP3		48	French Provincial Polished Rosewood	11,185	7,990
BP3T		48	Polished Ebony	10,865	7,790
BP3T		48	Polished Rosewood	11,185	7,990
BP5		49	Polished Ebony	11,505	8,190
BP5		49	Polished Rosewood	11,825	8,390
BPX5		49	Satin Mahogany	12,145	8,590
B252		52	Satin Ebony	14,165	9,590
Professional Series Grands					
BP148	4	10	Satin Ebony Lacquer	27,505	18,190
BP148	4	10	Polished Ebony	23,665	15,790
BP148	4	10	Polished Ebony with Silver Hardware	24,945	16,590
BP148	4	10	Polished Mahogany/Walnut/White	24,945	16,590
BP152	5		Satin Ebony Lacquer	30,705	20,190
BP152	5		Polished Ebony	26,865	17,790
BP152	5		Polished Mahogany/Walnut/White	28,145	18,590
BP165	5	5	Satin Ebony Lacquer	32,945	21,590
BP165	5	5	Polished Ebony	29,425	19,390
BP165	5	5	Polished Ebony with Silver Hardware	30,705	20,190
BP165	5	5	Polished Mahogany/Walnut/White	30,705	20,190
BP178	5	10	Satin Ebony Lacquer	43,825	28,390
BP178	5	10	Polished Ebony	39,665	25,790
BP178	5	10	Polished Mahogany/Walnut	41,265	26,790
BP190	6	3	Satin Ebony Lacquer	51,825	33,390
BP190	6	3	Polished Ebony	47,345	30,590
BP190	6	3	Polished Mahogany/Walnut	49,265	31,790
BP211	6	11	Polished Ebony	70,385	44,990
Academy Series Grands					
BA146	4	9	Satin Ebony	22,385	14,990
BA146	4	9	Polished Ebony	20,785	13,990
BA146	4	9	Polished Ebony with Silver Hardware	22,385	14,990
BA146	4	9	Polished Mahogany/Walnut/White	22,385	14,990
BA151	5		Satin Ebony	24,945	16,590
BA151	5		Polished Ebony	23,345	15,590
BA151	5		Polished Ebony with Silver Hardware	24,945	16,590
BA151	5		Polished Mahogany/Walnut/White	24,945	16,590
BA161	5	4	Satin Ebony	27,185	17,990
BA161	5	4	Polished Ebony	25,585	16,990
BA161	5	4	Polished Ebony with Silver Hardware	27,185	17,990
BA161	5	4	Polished Mahogany/Walnut/White	27,185	17,990

Model	Feet	Inches	Description	MSRP	SMP
BALDWIN *(continued)*					
BA177	5	9	Satin Ebony	33,585	21,990
BA177	5	9	Polished Ebony	31,985	20,990
BA177	5	9	Polished Mahogany/Walnut	33,585	21,990
BA186	6	1	Satin Ebony	39,985	25,990
BA186	6	1	Polished Ebony	38,385	24,990
BA217	7	1	Polished Ebony	51,185	32,990

BECHSTEIN, C.

C. Bechstein Academy Series Verticals

Model		Inches	Description	MSRP	SMP
A114 Modern		44	Polished Ebony	25,900	25,750
A114 Modern		44	Polished White	28,900	28,652
A114 Chrome Art		44	Polished Ebony	27,900	27,201
A114 Chrome Art		44	Polished White	29,900	29,628
A114 Compact		45.5	Polished Ebony	26,900	25,750
A114 Compact		45.5	Polished White	28,900	28,652
A116 Compact		45.5	Satin and Polished Walnut/Mahogany/Cherry	30,900	30,103
A124 Imposant		49	Polished Ebony	28,900	28,217
A124 Imposant		49	Polished White	31,900	31,119
A124 Style		49.5	Polished Ebony	29,900	29,668
A124 Style		49.5	Polished White	33,900	32,569
A124 Style		49.5	Satin and Polished Mahogany/Walnut/Cherry	34,900	34,020

C. Bechstein Verticals

Model		Inches	Description	MSRP	SMP
Millenium 116K		46	Polished Ebony	30,900	30,305
Millenium 116K		46	Polished White	33,900	33,418
Classic 118		46.5	Polished Ebony	32,900	31,861
Classic 118		46.5	Polished White	34,900	34,712
Classic 118		46.5	Satin and Polished Walnut/Mahogany/Cherry	36,900	36,531
Contour 118		46.5	Polished Ebony	33,900	33,418
Contour 118		46.5	Polished White	36,900	36,531
Contour 118		46.5	Satin and Polished Walnut/Mahogany/Cherry	37,900	37,798
Classic 124		49	Polished Ebony	38,900	38,087
Classic 124		49	Polished White	42,900	41,200
Classic 124		49	Satin and Polished Walnut/Mahogany/Cherry	43,900	42,757
Elegance 124		49	Polished Ebony	39,900	39,644
Elegance 124		49	Polished White	43,900	42,757
Elegance 124		49	Satin and Polished Walnut/Mahogany/Cherry	44,900	44,313
Concert 8		51.5	Polished Ebony	70,900	67,457
Concert 8		51.5	Polished White	73,900	68,969
Concert 8		51.5	Polished Walnut/Mahogany	76,900	70,481
Concert 8		51.5	Polished Burl Walnut	79,900	73,505
Concert 8		51.5	Polished Cherry w/Inlays	82,900	82,089

C. Bechstein Academy Series Grands

Model	Feet	Inches	Description	MSRP	SMP
A160	5	3	Polished Ebony	65,900	62,434
A160	5	3	Satin and Polished Mahogany/Walnut	75,900	73,330

PIANOBUYER *Model & Price Supplement*

Model	Feet	Inches	Description	MSRP	SMP

BECHSTEIN, C. *(continued)*

Model	Feet	Inches	Description	MSRP	SMP
A160	5	3	Polished White	72,900	69,104
A175	5	9	Polished Ebony	69,900	67,104
A175	5	9	Satin and Polished Walnut/Mahogany	79,900	77,999
A175	5	9	Polished White	76,900	73,773
A190	6	3	Polished Ebony	73,900	71,773
A190	6	3	Satin and Polished Mahogany/Walnut	83,900	82,669
A190	6	3	Polished White	79,900	76,443
A208	6	8	Polished Ebony	81,900	77,999
A208	6	8	Satin and Polished Mahogany/Walnut	91,900	91,564
A208	6	8	Polished White	88,900	84,669
A228	7	5	Polished Ebony	93,900	89,338
A228	7	5	Satin and Polished Mahogany/Walnut	103,900	103,617
A228	7	5	Polished White	99,900	95,564

C. Bechstein Grands

Model	Feet	Inches	Description	MSRP	SMP
L167	5	6	Polished Ebony	125,900	110,841
L167	5	6	Satin and Polished Mahogany/Walnut/Cherry	143,900	125,961
L167	5	6	Polished White	131,900	115,377
A192	6	4	Polished Ebony	148,900	130,498
A192	6	4	Satin and Polished Mahogany/Walnut/Cherry	166,900	145,618
A192	6	4	Polished White	156,900	138,058
B212	6	11	Polished Ebony	170,900	150,154
B212	6	11	Polished White	178,900	157,714
C234	7	7	Polished Ebony	199,900	167,094
C234	7	7	Polished White	219,900	175,551
D282	9	2	Polished Ebony	269,900	216,426
D282	9	2	Polished White	285,900	227,702

BLÜTHNER

Prices do not include bench.

Verticals

Model		Inches	Description	MSRP	SMP
D		45	Satin and Polished Ebony	34,648	32,356
D		45	Satin and Polished Walnut/Mahogany	37,420	34,864
D		45	Satin and Polished Cherry	37,594	35,022
D		45	Satin and Polished White	37,074	34,551
D		45	Satin and Polished Bubinga/Yew/Rosewood/Macassar	38,460	35,805
C		46	Satin and Polished Ebony	38,498	35,840
C		46	Satin and Polished Mahogany/Walnut	41,578	38,627
C		46	Satin and Polished Cherry	41,771	38,802
C		46	Satin and Polished White	41,193	38,279
C		46	Satin and Polished Bubinga/Yew/Rosewood/Macassar	42,733	39,672
C		46	Saxony Polished Pyramid Mahogany	48,893	45,247
C		46	Polished Burl Walnut/Camphor	51,973	48,034
A		49	Satin and Polished Ebony	44,357	41,142
A		49	Satin and Polished Mahogany/Walnut	47,905	44,353

Model	Feet	Inches	Description	MSRP	SMP
BLÜTHNER (continued)					
A		49	Satin and Polished Cherry	48,127	44,554
A		49	Satin and Polished White	47,462	43,952
A		49	Satin and Polished Bubinga/Yew/Rosewood/Macassar	49,236	45,557
A		49	Saxony Polished Pyramid Mahogany	56,333	51,980
A		49	Polished Burl Walnut/Camphor	59,882	55,192
B		52	Satin and Polished Ebony	50,215	46,443
B		52	Satin and Polished Mahogany/Walnut	54,232	50,079
B		52	Satin and Polished Cherry	54,483	50,306
B		52	Satin and Polished White	53,730	49,624
B		52	Satin and Polished Bubinga/Yew/Rosewood/Macassar	55,739	51,443
B		52	Saxony Polished Pyramid Mahogany	63,773	58,713
B		52	Polished Burl Walnut/Camphor	67,790	62,348
S		58	Satin and Polished Ebony	67,479	62,067
S		58	Satin and Polished Mahogany/Walnut	72,878	66,953
S		58	Satin and Polished Cherry	73,215	67,258
S		58	Satin and Polished White	72,203	66,342
S		58	Satin and Polished Bubinga/Yew/Rosewood/Macassar	74,902	68,785
S		58	Saxony Polished Pyramid Mahogany	85,699	78,556
S		58	Polished Burl Walnut/Camphor	91,097	83,441
Verticals			e-volution Hybrid Piano System, add	8,200	7,421
Verticals			Sostenuto, add	3,400	3,077
Grands					
11	5	1	Satin and Polished Ebony	86,874	79,619
11	5	1	Satin and Polished Mahogany/Walnut	93,824	85,909
11	5	1	Satin and Polished Cherry	94,258	86,301
11	5	1	Satin and Polished White	92,955	85,122
11	5	1	Satin and Polished Bubinga/Yew/Rosewood/Macassar	96,430	88,267
11	5	1	Saxony Polished Pyramid Mahogany	111,199	101,633
11	5	1	Polished Burl Walnut/Camphor	111,199	101,633
11	5	1	President Polished Ebony	98,462	90,106
11	5	1	President Polished Mahogany/Walnut	105,412	96,395
11	5	1	President Polished Bubinga	108,018	98,754
11	5	1	President Burl Walnut	122,787	112,119
11	5	1	Wilhelm II Satin and Polished Ebony	101,642	92,984
11	5	1	Wilhelm II Polished Mahogany/Walnut	109,774	100,343
11	5	1	Wilhelm II Polished Pyramid Mahogany	129,225	117,946
11	5	1	Wilhelm II Polished Burl Walnut	129,225	117,946
11	5	1	Ambassador Santos Rosewood	125,359	114,447
11	5	1	Ambassador Walnut	121,971	111,381
11	5	1	Nicolas II Satin Walnut with Burl Inlay	124,542	113,708
11	5	1	Louis XIV Rococo Satin White with Gold	139,433	127,184
11	5	1	Jubilee Polished Ebony	104,900	95,932
11	5	1	Jubilee Polished Mahogany/Walnut	111,850	102,222
11	5	1	Julius Bluthner Edition	107,837	98,590
11	5	1	Crystal Edition Elegance	131,979	120,438

Model	Feet	Inches	Description	MSRP	SMP
BLÜTHNER *(continued)*					
11	5	1	Crystal Edition Idyllic	154,512	140,830
PH	5	1	Paul Hennigsen Design	129,000	117,742
10	5	5	Satin and Polished Ebony	100,146	91,630
10	5	5	Satin and Polished Mahogany/Walnut	108,158	98,881
10	5	5	Satin and Polished Cherry	108,659	99,334
10	5	5	Satin and Polished White	107,156	97,974
10	5	5	Satin and Polished Bubinga/Yew/Rosewood/Macassar	111,162	101,599
10	5	5	Saxony Polished Pyramid Mahogany	126,184	115,194
10	5	5	Polished Burl Walnut/Camphor	126,184	115,194
10	5	5	President Polished Ebony	111,735	102,118
10	5	5	President Polished Mahogany/Walnut	119,746	109,367
10	5	5	President Polished Bubinga	122,751	112,087
10	5	5	President Burl Walnut	137,773	125,681
10	5	5	Senator Walnut w/Leather	115,884	105,872
10	5	5	Senator Jacaranda Satin Rosewood w/Leather	125,541	114,612
10	5	5	Wilhelm II Satin and Polished Ebony	117,171	107,037
10	5	5	Wilhelm II Polished Mahogany/Walnut	126,545	115,520
10	5	5	Wilhelm II Polished Pyramid Mahogany	144,211	131,508
10	5	5	Wilhelm II Polished Burl Walnut	144,211	131,508
10	5	5	Ambassador Santos Rosewood	144,511	131,779
10	5	5	Ambassador Walnut	140,605	128,244
10	5	5	Nicolas II Satin Walnut with Burl Inlay	138,803	126,614
10	5	5	Louis XIV Rococo Satin White with Gold	160,735	146,462
10	5	5	Jubilee Polished Ebony	118,173	107,944
10	5	5	Jubilee Polished Mahogany/Walnut	126,184	115,194
10	5	5	Dynasty	144,211	131,508
10	5	5	Julius Bluthner Edition	119,103	108,786
10	5	5	Crystal Edition Elegance	144,855	132,090
10	5	5	Crystal Edition Idyllic	167,388	152,482
PH	5	9	Paul Hennigsen Design	169,000	153,941
6	6	3	Satin and Polished Ebony	113,868	104,048
6	6	3	Satin and Polished Mahogany/Walnut	122,977	112,291
6	6	3	Satin and Polished Cherry	123,546	112,806
6	6	3	Satin and Polished White	121,838	111,261
6	6	3	Satin and Polished Bubinga/Yew/Rosewood/Macassar	126,393	115,383
6	6	3	Saxony Polished Pyramid Mahogany	143,473	130,840
6	6	3	Polished Burl Walnut/Camphor	143,473	130,840
6	6	3	President Polished Ebony	125,456	114,535
6	6	3	President Polished Mahogany/Walnut	134,565	122,778
6	6	3	President Polished Bubinga	137,981	125,870
6	6	3	President Burl Walnut	155,062	141,328
6	6	3	Senator Walnut w/Leather	128,760	117,525
6	6	3	Senator Jacaranda Satin Rosewood w/Leather	138,417	126,264
6	6	3	Wilhelm II Satin and Polished Ebony	133,225	121,566
6	6	3	Wilhelm II Polished Mahogany/Walnut	143,883	131,211

Model	Feet	Inches	Description	MSRP	SMP
BLÜTHNER *(continued)*					
6	6	3	Wilhelm II Polished Pyramid Mahogany	161,500	147,154
6	6	3	Wilhelm II Polished Burl Walnut	161,500	147,154
6	6	3	Ambassador Santos Rosewood	156,727	142,834
6	6	3	Ambassador Walnut	153,721	140,114
6	6	3	Nicolas II Satin Walnut with Burl Inlay	157,821	143,824
6	6	3	Louis XIV Rococo Satin White with Gold	182,758	166,392
6	6	3	Jubilee Polished Ebony	131,894	120,361
6	6	3	Jubilee Polished Mahogany/Walnut	141,003	128,605
6	6	3	Dynasty	161,500	147,154
6	6	3	Julius Bluthner Edition	125,874	114,913
6	6	3	Crystal Edition Elegance	159,840	145,652
6	6	3	Crystal Edition Idyllic	199,800	181,814
6	6	3	Jubilee Plate, add	5,794	5,243
4	6	10	Satin and Polished Ebony	133,962	122,233
4	6	10	Satin and Polished Mahogany/Walnut	144,679	131,931
4	6	10	Satin and Polished Cherry	145,349	132,538
4	6	10	Satin and Polished White	143,339	130,719
4	6	10	Satin and Polished Bubinga/Yew/Rosewood/Macassar	148,698	135,568
4	6	10	Saxony Polished Pyramid Mahogany	168,792	153,753'
4	6	10	Polished Burl Walnut/Camphor	168,792	153,753
4	6	10	President Polished Ebony	145,550	132,719
4	6	10	President Polished Mahogany/Walnut	156,267	142,418
4	6	10	President Polished Bubinga	160,286	146,055
4	6	10	President Burl Walnut	180,380	164,240
4	6	10	Senator Walnut w/Leather	148,074	135,004
4	6	10	Senator Jacaranda Satin Rosewood w/Leather	157,731	143,743
4	6	10	Wilhelm II Satin and Polished Ebony	156,735	142,842
4	6	10	Wilhelm II Polished Mahogany/Walnut	169,274	154,189
4	6	10	Wilhelm II Polished Pyramid Mahogany	186,818	170,066
4	6	10	Wilhelm II Polished Burl Walnut	186,818	170,066
4	6	10	Ambassador Santos Rosewood	181,411	165,173
4	6	10	Ambassador Walnut	176,508	160,736
4	6	10	Nicolas II Satin Walnut with Burl Inlay	185,671	169,028
4	6	10	Louis XIV Rococo Satin White with Gold	215,009	195,578
4	6	10	Jubilee Polished Ebony	151,988	138,546
4	6	10	Jubilee Polished Mahogany/Walnut	162,705	148,244
4	6	10	Dynasty	186,818	170,066
4	6	10	Julius Bluthner Edition	152,903	139,374
4	6	10	Queen Victoria JB Edition Polished Rosewood	183,000	166,611
4	6	10	Crystal Edition Elegance	177,045	161,222
4	6	10	Crystal Edition Idyllic	218,892	199,092
2	7	8	Satin and Polished Ebony	150,707	137,386
2	7	8	Satin and Polished Mahogany/Walnut	162,764	148,298
2	7	8	Satin and Polished Cherry	163,517	148,979
2	7	8	Satin and Polished White	161,257	146,934

PIANOBUYER *Model & Price Supplement*

Model	Feet	Inches	Description	MSRP	SMP
BLÜTHNER *(continued)*					
2	7	8	Satin and Polished Bubinga/Yew/Rosewood/Macassar	167,285	152,389
2	7	8	Saxony Polished Pyramid Mahogany	191,398	174,211
2	7	8	Polished Burl Walnut/Camphor	191,398	174,211
2	7	8	President Polished Ebony	162,296	147,874
2	7	8	President Polished Mahogany/Walnut	174,352	158,785
2	7	8	President Polished Bubinga	178,873	162,876
2	7	8	President Burl Walnut	202,986	184,698
2	7	8	Senator Walnut w/Leather	160,950	146,656
2	7	8	Senator Jacaranda Satin Rosewood w/Leather	170,607	155,395
2	7	8	Wilhelm II Satin and Polished Ebony	176,327	160,572
2	7	8	Wilhelm II Polished Mahogany/Walnut	190,434	173,338
2	7	8	Wilhelm II Polished Pyramid Mahogany	209,424	190,524
2	7	8	Wilhelm II Polished Burl Walnut	209,424	190,524
2	7	8	Ambassador Santos Rosewood	204,088	185,695
2	7	8	Ambassador Walnut	198,572	180,703
2	7	8	Nicolas II Satin Walnut with Burl Inlay	210,538	191,532
2	7	8	Louis XIV Rococo Satin White with Gold	241,885	219,900
2	7	8	Jubilee Polished Ebony	168,734	153,700
2	7	8	Jubilee Polished Mahogany/Walnut	180,790	164,611
2	7	8	Dynasty	209,424	190,524
2	7	8	Julius Bluthner Edition	177,045	161,222
2	7	8	Queen Victoria JB Edition Polished Rosewood	202,456	184,218
2	7	8	Crystal Edition Elegance	231,768	210,745
2	7	8	Crystal Edition Idyllic	273,615	248,615
1	9	2	Satin and Polished Ebony	203,253	184,939
1	9	2	Satin and Polished Mahogany/Walnut	219,513	199,654
1	9	2	Satin and Polished Cherry	220,529	200,574
1	9	2	Satin and Polished White	217,480	197,814
1	9	2	Satin and Polished Bubinga/Yew/Rosewood/Macassar	225,610	205,172
1	9	2	Saxony Polished Pyramid Mahogany	258,131	234,603
1	9	2	Polished Burl Walnut/Camphor	264,228	240,120
1	9	2	President Polished Ebony	216,040	196,511
1	9	2	President Polished Mahogany/Walnut	232,300	211,226
1	9	2	President Polished Bubinga	238,398	216,745
1	9	2	President Burl Walnut	277,016	251,693
1	9	2	Wilhelm II Satin and Polished Ebony	237,805	216,208
1	9	2	Wilhelm II Polished Mahogany/Walnut	256,830	233,425
1	9	2	Wilhelm II Polished Pyramid Mahogany	278,022	252,604
1	9	2	Wilhelm II Polished Burl Walnut	284,120	258,122
1	9	2	Ambassador Santos Rosewood	279,757	254,174
1	9	2	Ambassador Walnut	274,391	249,318
1	9	2	Nicolas II Satin Walnut with Burl Inlay	290,651	264,033
1	9	2	Jubilee Polished Ebony	223,144	202,940
1	9	2	Jubilee Polished Mahogany/Walnut	239,404	217,655
1	9	2	Dynasty	288,600	262,176

Model	Feet	Inches	Description	MSRP	SMP
BLÜTHNER *(continued)*					
1	9	2	Julius Bluthner Edition	230,798	209,867
1	9	2	Queen Victoria JB Edition Polished Rosewood	244,938	222,663
1	9	2	Crystal Edition Elegance	273,060	248,113
1	9	2	Crystal Edition Idyllic	316,350	287,290
Grands			e-volution Hybrid Piano System, add	8,800	7,964

BÖSENDORFER

Verticals

Model	Feet	Inches	Description	MSRP	SMP
130		52	Satin and Polished Ebony	76,999	72,998
130		52	Satin and Polished White, other colors	91,999	86,998
130		52	Polished, Satin, Open-pore: Walnut, Cherry, Mahogany, Pomele	98,999	92,998
130		52	Polished , Satin, Open-pore: Pyramid Mahogany, Burl Walnut, Birdseye Maple, Macassar, Madronna, Vavona, Wenge	103,999	98,998

Grands

Model	Feet	Inches	Description	MSRP	SMP
155	5	1	Satin and Polished Ebony	121,999	114,998
155	5	1	Satin and Polished White, other colors	136,999	128,998
155	5	1	Polished, Satin, Open-pore: Walnut, Cherry, Mahogany, Pomele	146,999	138,998
155	5	1	Polished , Satin, Open-pore: Pyramid Mahogany, Burl Walnut, Birdseye Maple, Macassar, Madronna, Vavona, Wenge	159,999	150,998
155	5	1	Chrome: Satin and Polished Ebony	138,999	130,998
170VC	5	7	Satin and Polished Ebony	126,999	120,998
170VC	5	7	Satin and Polished White, other colors	142,999	134,998
170VC	5	7	Polished, Satin, Open-pore: Walnut, Cherry, Mahogany, Pomele	153,999	144,998
170VC	5	7	Polished , Satin, Open-pore: Bubinga, Pyramid Mahogany, Santos Rosewood, Burl Walnut, Birdseye Maple, Macassar, Madronna, Vavona, Wenge	164,999	154,998
170VC	5	7	Chrome: Satin and Polished Ebony	142,999	134,998
170VC	5	7	Johann Strauss: Satin and Polished Ebony w/Maple	152,999	144,998
170VC	5	7	Johann Strauss: Any finish and veneer	178,999	168,998
170VC	5	7	Liszt: Polished Vavona	182,999	172,998
170VC	5	7	Chopin, Louis XVI: Satin Pommele	207,999	196,998
170VC	5	7	Baroque: Light Satin Ivory; Vienna: Polished Amboyna	232,999	218,998
170VC	5	7	Artisan Satin and Polished	297,999	280,998
185VC CS	6	1	Conservatory Satin Ebony	116,999	110,998
185VC	6	1	Satin and Polished Ebony	133,999	126,998
185VC	6	1	Satin and Polished White, other colors	149,999	140,998
185VC	6	1	Polished, Satin, Open-pore: Walnut, Cherry, Mahogany, Pomele	157,999	148,998
185VC	6	1	Polished , Satin, Open-pore: Pyramid Mahogany, Burl Walnut, Birdseye Maple, Macassar, Madronna, Vavona, Wenge	169,999	160,998

Model	Feet	Inches	Description	MSRP	SMP

BÖSENDORFER (continued)

Model	Feet	Inches	Description	MSRP	SMP
185VC	6	1	Chrome: Satin and Polished Ebony	149,999	140,998
185VC	6	1	Johann Strauss: Satin and Polished Ebony w/Maple	159,999	150,998
185VC	6	1	Johann Strauss: Any finish and veneer	185,000	174,998
185VC	6	1	Liszt: Polished Vavona	189,999	178,998
185VC	6	1	Edge: Satin and Polished Ebony	212,999	200,998
185VC	6	1	Chopin, Louis XVI: Satin Pommele	215,999	202,998
185VC	6	1	Baroque: Satin Light Ivory; Vienna: Polished Amboyna	236,999	222,998
185VC	6	1	Porsche Design: Diamond Black Metallic Gloss	248,999	234,998
185VC	6	1	Artisan Satin and Polished	306,999	288,998
200CS	6	7	Conservatory Satin Ebony	122,999	116,998
200	6	7	Satin and Polished Ebony	144,999	136,998
200	6	7	Satin and Polished White, other colors	161,999	152,998
200	6	7	Polished, Satin, Open-pore: Walnut, Cherry, Mahogany, Pomele	172,999	162,998
200	6	7	Polished , Satin, Open-pore: Pyramid Mahogany, Burl Walnut, Birdseye Maple, Macassar, Madronna, Vavona, Wenge	185,999	174,998
200	6	7	Chrome Satin and Polished Ebony	145,596	120,744
200	6	7	Chrome: Satin and Polished Ebony	159,999	150,998
200	6	7	Johann Strauss: Satin and Polished Ebony w/Maple	170,999	160,998
200	6	7	Johann Strauss: Any finish and veneer	201,999	190,998
200	6	7	Dragonfly: Maple and Polished Ebony	206,999	194,998
200	6	7	Liszt: Polished Vavona	206,999	194,998
200	6	7	Beethoven Polished Ebony, Klimt "Woman in Gold"	176,999	166,998
200	6	7	Beethoven: Chrome; Cocteau: White	204,999	192,998
200	6	7	Edge: Satin and Polished Ebony	233,999	220,998
200	6	7	Chopin, Louis XVI: Satin Pommele	236,999	222,998
200	6	7	Baroque: Satin Light Ivory; Vienna: Polished Amboyna	259,999	244,998
200	6	7	Artisan Satin and Polished	325,999	306,998
214VC CS	7		Conservatory Satin Ebony	132,999	126,998
214VC	7		Satin and Polished Ebony	158,999	150,998
214VC	7		Satin and Polished White, other colors	181,999	170,998
214VC	7		Polished, Satin, Open-pore: Walnut, Cherry, Mahogany, Pomele	193,999	182,998
214VC	7		Polished , Satin, Open-pore: Pyramid Mahogany, Burl Walnut, Birdseye Maple, Macassar, Madronna, Vavona, Wenge	211,999	198,998
214VC	7		Chrome: Satin and Polished Ebony	180,999	170,998
214VC	7		Johann Strauss: Satin and Polished Ebony w/Maple	189,999	178,998
214VC	7		Johann Strauss: Any finish and veneer	227,999	214,998
214VC	7		Liszt: Polished Vavona	233,999	220,998
214VC	7		Beethoven: Polished Ebony, Klimt "Woman in Gold"	191,999	182,998
214VC	7		Beethoven: Chrome; Cocteau: White	225,999	212,998
214VC	7		Edge: Satin and Polished Ebony	258,999	246,998
214VC	7		Chopin, Louis XVI: Satin Pommele	266,999	250,998
214VC	7		Baroque: Satin Light Ivory; Vienna: Polished Amboyna	292,999	274,998
214VC	7		Porsche Design: Diamond Black Metallic Gloss	308,999	290,998

Model	Feet	Inches	Description	MSRP	SMP
BÖSENDORFER *(continued)*					
214VC	7		Audi Design Polished Ebony	372,999	352,998
214VC	7		Artisan Satin and Polished	372,999	352,998
225	7	4	Satin and Polished Ebony	178,999	168,998
225	7	4	Satin and Polished White, other colors	197,999	186,998
225	7	4	Polished, Satin, Open-pore: Walnut, Cherry, Mahogany, Pomele	212,999	200,998
225	7	4	Polished , Satin, Open-pore: Pyramid Mahogany, Burl Walnut, Birdseye Maple, Macassar, Madronna, Vavona, Wenge	229,999	216,998
225	7	4	Chrome: Satin and Polished Ebony	193,999	182,999
225	7	4	Johann Strauss: Satin and Polished Ebony w/Maple	204,999	192,998
225	7	4	Johann Strauss: Any finish and veneer	248,999	234,998
225	7	4	Liszt: Polished Vavona	255,999	240,998
225	7	4	Chopin, Louis XVI: Satin Pommele	291,999	274,998
225	7	4	Baroque: Satin Light Ivory; Vienna: Polished Amboyna	319,999	300,998
225	7	4	Artisan Satin and Polished	398,999	374,998
225	7	4	Grand Bohemian: Polished Ebony	420,000	420,000
280VC	9	2	Satin and Polished Ebony	229,999	216,998
280VC	9	2	Satin and Polished White, other colors	254,999	240,998
280VC	9	2	Polished, Satin, Open-pore: Walnut, Cherry, Mahogany, Pomele	274,999	258,998
280VC	9	2	Polished , Satin, Open-pore: Pyramid Mahogany, Burl Walnut, Birdseye Maple, Macassar, Madronna, Vavona, Wenge	297,999	280,998
280VC	9	2	Johann Strauss: Satin and Polished Ebony w/Maple	270,999	254,998
280VC	9	2	Johann Strauss: Any finish and veneer	323,999	304,998
280VC	9	2	Liszt: Polished Vavona	331,999	312,998
280VC	9	2	Chopin, Louis XVI: Satin Pommele	379,999	356,998
280VC	9	2	Baroque: Satin Light Ivory; Vienna: Polished Amboyna	412,999	390,998
280VC	9	2	Porsche Design: Diamond Black Metallic Gloss	437,999	412,998
280VC	9	2	Artisan Satin and Polished	472,999	444,998
290	9	6	Satin and Polished Ebony	262,999	246,998
290	9	6	Satin and Polished White, other colors	288,999	272,998
290	9	6	Polished, Satin, Open-pore: Walnut, Cherry, Mahogany, Pomele	312,999	294,998
290	9	6	Polished , Satin, Open-pore: Pyramid Mahogany, Burl Walnut, Birdseye Maple, Macassar, Madronna, Vavona, Wenge	338,999	318,998
290	9	6	Johann Strauss: Satin and Polished Ebony w/Maple	302,999	284,998
290	9	6	Johann Strauss: Any finish and veneer	369,999	346,998
290	9	6	Liszt: Polished Vavona	377,999	354,998
290	9	6	Chopin, Louis XVI: Satin Pommele	429,999	404,998
290	9	6	Baroque: Satin Light Ivory; Vienna: Polished Amboyna	472,999	444,998
290	9	6	Artisan Satin and Polished	536,999	506,998
Select models			Disklavier Enspire PRO, add	39,999	37,998

Model	Feet	Inches	Description	MSRP	SMP

BOSTON

Boston MSRP is the price at the New York retail store.

Verticals

Model	Feet	Inches	Description	MSRP	SMP
UP-118E PE		46	Satin and Polished Ebony	12,300	12,300
UP-118E PE		46	Polished Mahogany	14,200	14,200
UP-118E PE		46	Satin and Polished Walnut	14,200	14,200
UP-118S PE		46	Satin Black Oak	8,100	8,100
UP-120S PE-II		48	Polished Ebony	8,200	8,200
UP-120S PE-II		48	Satin Walnut	9,700	9,700
UP-126E PE		50	Polished Ebony	14,700	14,700
UP-126E PE		50	Polished Mahogany	17,100	17,100
UP-132E PE		52	Polished Ebony	16,400	16,400
UP-132E PE		52	Polished Ebony	15,900	15,900

Grands

Model	Feet	Inches	Description	MSRP	SMP
GP-156 PE-II	5	1	Satin and Polished Ebony	22,600	22,600
GP-163 PE-II	5	4	Satin and Polished Ebony	27,400	27,400
GP-163 PE-II	5	4	Satin and Polished Mahogany	30,100	30,100
GP-163 PE-II	5	4	Satin and Polished Walnut	30,400	30,400
GP-163 PE-II	5	4	Polished White	33,800	33,800
GP-178 PE-II	5	10	Satin and Polished Ebony	32,100	32,100
GP-178A PE-II	5	10	Polished Ebony with Silver Hardware	33,900	33,900
GP-178 PE-II	5	10	Satin and Polished Mahogany	34,600	34,600
GP-178 PE-II	5	10	Satin and Polished Walnut	35,100	35,100
GP-193 PE-II	6	4	Satin and Polished Ebony	41,700	41,700
GP-215 PE-II	7	1	Polished Ebony	54,500	54,500

BRODMANN

Verticals

Model	Feet	Inches	Description	MSRP	SMP
CE 118		47	Polished Ebony	10,290	6,580
PE 118V		47	Vienna Polished Ebony	13,990	8,580
PE 121		48	Polished Ebony	12,890	7,980
PE 121		48	Polished Mahogany/Walnut	13,990	8,580
PE 121		48	Polished White	14,390	8,780
PE 121		48	Polished Two Tone (Apple Tree Saphire/Ebony)	15,490	9,380
PE 124V		48	Vienna Polished Ebony	16,190	9,780
PE 124V		48	Vienna Polished Bubinga	17,290	10,380
PE 126I		49	Polished Ebony w/Institutional Wide Music Desk	15,790	9,580
PE 130		52	Polished Ebony	19,890	11,780
PE 132V		52	Vienna Polished Ebony	21,390	12,580
AS 132		52	Polished Ebony	29,490	16,980
AS 132		52	Polished Ebony	29,490	16,980

Grands

Model	Feet	Inches	Description	MSRP	SMP
CE 148	4	10	Polished Ebony	25,390	14,780
CE 175	5	9	Polished Ebony	29,490	16,980
PE 150	5		Polished Ebony	30,190	17,380
PE 162	5	4	Polished Ebony	35,390	20,180

Model	Feet	Inches	Description	MSRP	SMP
BRODMANN *(continued)*					
PE 162	5	4	Polished Mahogany/Walnut/Walnut Burst	39,090	22,180
PE 162	5	4	Polished White	37,590	21,380
PE 162	5	4	Polished Bubinga	39,390	22,380
PE 162	5	4	Polished Two Tone (Ebony/Bubinga)	36,090	20,580
PE 162	5	4	Polished Two Tone (Apple Tree Saphire/Ebony)	39,090	22,180
PE 187	6	2	Polished Ebony	40,190	22,780
PE 187 V	6	2	Polished Ebony w/Carbon-Fiber Action	46,790	26,380
PE 187	6	2	Polished Mahogany/Walnut	43,890	24,780
PE 187	6	2	Polished White	43,090	24,380
PE 187	6	2	Polished Bubinga	45,290	25,580
PE 187	6	2	Strauss Polished Ebony	43,090	24,380
PE 187	6	2	Strauss Polished Two Tone (Ebony/Bubinga)	44,190	24,980
PE 212	7		Polished Ebony	63,390	35,380
PE 228	7	5	Polished Ebony	82,590	45,780
AS 188	6	2	Polished Ebony	66,990	45,660
AS 211	7		Polished Ebony	84,990	57,660
AS 227	7	6	Polished Ebony	96,990	65,660
AS 275	9		Polished Ebony	159,990	86,980
Grands			With Carbon-Fiber Action, add	6,600	3,600

CLINE

Verticals

Model	Feet	Inches	Description	MSRP	SMP
CL118		46.5	Polished Ebony		6,900
CL118		46.5	Polished Ebony w/Nickel		7,300
CL118		46.5	Polished Walnut/Mahogany		7,300
CL121/123		48	Polished Ebony		7,100
CL121/123		48	Polished Ebony w/Nickel		8,700
CL121/123		48	Polished Mahogany/Walnut		8,700
CL121/123		48	Polished Mahogany/Walnut w/Detail Trim		7,590

Grands

Model	Feet	Inches	Description	MSRP	SMP
CL 150	4	11	Polished Ebony		14,300

CRISTOFORI

Verticals

Model	Feet	Inches	Description	MSRP	SMP
V450		45	Polished Ebony	4,299	4,299
V450		45	Polished Mahogany	4,499	4,499
V465		46.5	Polished Ebony	4,699	4,512
V465		46.5	Polished Mahogany	4,899	4,738
V480LS		48	Polished Ebony	5,499	5,054
V480LS		48	Polished Mahogany	5,699	5,280
V480LS		48	Polished Mahogany	5,199	4,668

Model	Feet	Inches	Description	MSRP	SMP

CRISTOFORI *(continued)*

Grands

Model	Feet	Inches	Description	MSRP	SMP
G410L	4	10	Polished Ebony	9,490	9,342
G410L	4	10	Polished Mahogany	9,790	9,758
G53L	5	3	Satin Ebony	10,690	10,224
G53L	5	3	Polished Ebony	10,490	9,808
G53L	5	3	Polished Mahogany/Snow White	10,790	10,224
G57L	5	7	Satin Ebony	12,190	11,836
G57L	5	7	Polished Ebony	11,990	11,432
G57L	5	7	Polished Mahogany	12,290	11,836
G62L	6	2	Satin Ebony	14,290	14,290
G62L	6	2	Polished Ebony	13,990	13,978

CUNNINGHAM

Verticals

Model	Inches	Description	MSRP	SMP
Studio Upright	48	Satin Ebony	9,890	9,890
Studio Upright	48	Polished Ebony	9,290	9,290
Studio Upright	48	Satin Mahogany	10,290	10,290
Studio Upright	48	Polished Mahogany	9,690	9,690

Grands

Model	Feet	Inches	Description	MSRP	SMP
Baby Grand	5		Satin Ebony	22,490	22,490
Baby Grand	5		Polished Ebony	21,290	21,290
Baby Grand	5		Satin Mahogany	23,190	23,190
Baby Grand	5		Polished Mahogany	21,990	21,990
Studio Grand	5	4	Satin Ebony	25,090	25,090
Studio Grand	5	4	Polished Ebony	23,890	23,890
Studio Grand	5	4	Satin Mahogany	25,790	25,790
Studio Grand	5	4	Polished Mahogany	24,590	24,590
Parlour Grand	5	10	Satin Ebony	30,490	30,490
Parlour Grand	5	10	Polished Ebony	29,290	29,290
Parlour Grand	5	10	Satin Mahogany	31,190	31,190
Parlour Grand	5	10	Polished Mahogany	29,990	29,990
Chamber Grand	7		Satin Ebony	46,290	46,290
Chamber Grand	7		Polished Ebony	44,790	44,790
Concert Grand	9		Satin Ebony	70,990	70,990
Concert Grand	9		Polished Ebony	68,990	68,990

DISKLAVIER — see Yamaha; see also Bösendorfer

EMERSON

Verticals

Model	Inches	Description	MSRP	SMP
EM8	51	Polished Ebony	25,254	15,836

Model	Feet	Inches	Description	MSRP	SMP

EMERSON (continued)

Grands

Model	Feet	Inches	Description	MSRP	SMP
EM168	5	6	Polished Ebony	59,442	38,628
EM180	5	11	Polished Ebony	69,861	45,574

ESSEX

Essex MSRP is the price at the New York retail store.

Verticals

Model	Inches	Description	MSRP	SMP
EUP-108C	42	Continental Polished Ebony	5,890	5,890
EUP-111E	44	Polished Ebony	6,590	6,590
EUP-111E	44	Polished Sapele Mahogany	6,990	6,700
EUP-116E	45	Polished Ebony	7,390	6,940
EUP-116E	45	Polished Sapele Mahogany	7,690	7,040
EUP-116E	45	Polished White	7,990	7,280
EUP-116CT	45	Contemporary Satin Lustre Sapele Mahogany	8,490	7,800
EUP-116QA	45	Queen Anne Satin Lustre Cherry	8,190	7,940
EUP-116EC	45	English Country Satin Lustre Walnut	8,190	7,760
EUP-116FF	45	Formal French Satin Lustre Brown Cherry	8,490	7,980
EUP-123E	48	Satin Ebony w/Chrome Hardware	8,890	8,180
EUP-123E	48	Polished Ebony	7,890	7,480
EUP-123E	48	Polished Ebony w/Chrome Hardware	7,990	7,600
EUP-123E	48	Polished Sapele Mahogany	8,990	8,000
EUP-123FL	48	Empire Satin Walnut	9,100	8,060
EUP-123FL	48	Empire Satin Sapele Mahogany	9,100	8,300
EUP-123S	48	Institutional Studio Polished Ebony	7,890	7,820

Grands

Model	Feet	Inches	Description	MSRP	SMP
EGP-155	5	1	Satin and Polished Ebony	14,300	14,300
EGP-155	5	1	Polished Sapele Mahogany	15,700	15,700
EGP-155	5	1	Polished White	19,200	16,940
EGP-155F	5	1	French Provincial Satin Lustre Brown Cherry	18,200	18,120
EGP-173	5	8	Polished Ebony	18,100	18,100

ESTONIA

The Estonia factory can make custom-designed finishes with exotic veneers; prices upon request.
Prices here include Jansen adjustable artist benches.

Grands

Model	Feet	Inches	Description	MSRP	SMP
L168	5	6	Satin and Polished Ebony	43,800	41,538
L168	5	6	Satin and Polished Mahogany/Walnut	47,380	44,641
L168	5	6	Polished Kewazinga Bubinga	51,395	48,564
L168	5	6	Polished Pyramid Mahogany	56,873	53,814
L168	5	6	Satin and Polished White	49,880	46,927
L168	5	6	Hidden Beauty Polished Ebony w/Bubinga	48,473	45,603
L190	6	3	Satin and Polished Ebony	53,789	50,496

Model	Feet	Inches	Description	MSRP	SMP

ESTONIA *(continued)*

Model	Feet	Inches	Description	MSRP	SMP
L190	6	3	Satin and Polished Mahogany/Walnut	57,298	54,212
L190	6	3	Polished Pyramid Mahogany	68,400	63,318
L190	6	3	Polished Santos Rosewood	68,400	63,146
L190	6	3	Polished Kewazinga Bubinga	61,688	58,256
L190	6	3	Hidden Beauty Polished Ebony w/Bubinga	56,570	53,399
L210	6	10	Satin and Polished Ebony	63,300	60,796
L210	6	10	Satin and Polished Mahogany/Walnut/White	69,630	66,778
L210	6	10	Polished Pyramid Mahogany	79,125	75,746
L210	6	10	Polished Kewazinga Bubinga	74,700	71,560
L210	6	10	Hidden Beauty Polished Ebony w/Bubinga	67,230	64,293
L225	7	4	Satin and Polished Ebony	79,689	74,297
L225	7	4	Satin and Polished Mahogany/Walnut/White	85,727	80,667
L225	7	4	Polished Pyramid Mahogany	95,156	90,710
L225	7	4	Polished Kewazinga Bubinga	86,100	83,597
L225	7	4	Hidden Beauty Polished Ebony w/Bubinga	84,635	79,451
L274	9		Satin and Polished Ebony	127,140	112,678
L274	9		Satin and Polished Mahogany/Walnut	139,430	124,475
L274	9		Polished Pyramid Mahogany	144,254	137,514
L274	9		Satin and Polished White	131,177	119,193

FANDRICH & SONS

These are the prices on the Fandrich & Sons website. Other finishes available at additional cost. See website for details.

Verticals

Model	Feet	Inches	Description	MSRP	SMP
EU131-V		52	Polished Ebony	12,990	12,990

Grands

Model	Feet	Inches	Description	MSRP	SMP
160-S	5	3	Polished Ebony	14,650	14,650
170-S	5	7	Polished Ebony	16,995	16,995
212-E	7		Polished Ebony	26,890	26,890

FAZIOLI

Fazioli is willing to make custom-designed cases with exotic veneers, marquetry, and other embellishments. Prices on request to Fazioli.

Grands

Model	Feet	Inches	Description	MSRP	SMP
F156	5	2	Satin and Polished Ebony	121,200	115,091
F156	5	2	Satin and Polished White/Red	139,400	131,934
F156	5	2	Satin and Polished Walnut/Cherry/Mahogany	151,500	142,828
F156	5	2	Satin and Polished Pyramid Mahogany/Macassar	169,700	159,443
F156	5	2	Satin and Polished Briers: Mahogany/California Walnut/ Sequoia	181,800	170,338
F156	5	2	Satin and Polished Olive	193,300	181,702
F183	6		Satin and Polished Ebony	125,400	118,974
F183	6		Satin and Polished White/Red	142,700	134,580
F183	6		Satin and Polished Walnut/Cherry/Mahogany	155,100	145,926

Model	Feet	Inches	Description	MSRP	SMP

FAZIOLI (continued)

Model	Feet	Inches	Description	MSRP	SMP
F183	6		Satin and Polished Pyramid Mahogany/Macassar	173,800	162,765
F183	6		Satin and Polished Briers: Mahogany/California Walnut/ Sequoia	186,100	174,112
F183	6		Satin and Polished Olive	197,200	185,368
F212	7		Satin and Polished Ebony	143,600	136,444
F212	7		Satin and Polished White/Red	154,800	146,434
F212	7		Satin and Polished Walnut/Cherry/Mahogany	168,900	159,082
F212	7		Satin and Polished Pyramid Mahogany/Macassar	183,000	171,825
F212	7		Satin and Polished Briers: Mahogany/California Walnut/ Sequoia	197,000	184,476
F212	7		Satin and Polished Olive	208,800	196,272
F228	7	6	Satin and Polished Ebony	161,400	153,850
F228	7	6	Satin and Polished White/Red	174,000	165,117
F228	7	6	Satin and Polished Walnut/Cherry/Mahogany	189,800	179,762
F228	7	6	Satin and Polished Pyramid Mahogany/Macassar	205,700	194,174
F228	7	6	Satin and Polished Briers: Mahogany/California Walnut/ Sequoia	221,500	208,587
F228	7	6	Satin and Polished Olive	247,400	225,982
F278	9	2	Satin and Polished Ebony	217,900	204,917
F278	9	2	Satin and Polished White/Red	232,700	218,223
F278	9	2	Satin and Polished Walnut/Cherry/Mahogany	253,900	237,450
F278	9	2	Satin and Polished Pyramid Mahogany/Macassar	275,000	256,680
F278	9	2	Satin and Polished Briers: Mahogany/California Walnut/ Sequoia	296,200	275,908
F278	9	2	Satin and Polished Olive	315,700	293,601
F308	10	2	Satin and Polished Ebony	238,300	220,070
F308	10	2	Satin and Polished White/Red	254,500	234,495
F308	10	2	Satin and Polished Walnut/Cherry/Mahogany	277,600	255,157
F308	10	2	Satin and Polished Pyramid Mahogany/Macassar	300,800	275,583
F308	10	2	Satin and Polished Briers: Mahogany/California Walnut/ Sequoia	323,800	295,921
F308	10	2	Satin and Polished Olive	336,600	306,306

FÖRSTER, AUGUST

Prices do not include bench. Euro = $1.14

Verticals

Model		Inches	Description		SMP
116 C		46	Chippendale Satin Ebony		31,543
116 C		46	Chippendale Satin Walnut		33,535
116 D		46	Continental Satin Ebony		21,815
116 D		46	Continental Polished Ebony		24,149
116 D		46	Continental Satin Mahogany/Walnut/Oak/Cherry		23,949
116 D		46	Continental Polished Mahogany/Walnut		26,456
116 D		46	Continental Satin Beech		22,235
116 D		46	Continental Polished White with bench		26,220
116 E		46	Satin Ebony		26,036
116 E		46	Polished Ebony		28,265

Model	Feet	Inches	Description	MSRP	SMP
FÖRSTER, AUGUST *(continued)*					
116 E		46	Satin Mahogany/Walnut/Oak/Cherry		28,085
116 E		46	Polished Mahogany/Walnut		30,546
116 E		46	Satin Beech		26,456
116 E		46	Polished White with bench		30,337
125 F		49	Polished Ebony		32,618
125 G		49	Satin Ebony		29,681
125 G		49	Polished Ebony		31,936
125 G		49	Satin Mahogany/Walnut/Oak/Cherry		32,306
125 G		49	Polished Mahogany/Walnut		34,951
125 G		49	Satin Beech		30,101
125 G		49	Polished White with bench		34,427
125 G		49	With Oval Medallion, add		1,600
134 K		53	Polished Ebony		49,661
125 G		49	With Oval Medallion, add		1,600
134 K		53	Polished Ebony		49,661
Grands					
170	5	8	Satin Ebony		62,194
170	5	8	Polished Ebony		66,573
170	5	8	Satin Mahogany/Walnut/Cherry		66,415
170	5	8	Polished Mahogany/Walnut		70,584
170	5	8	Polished White with bench		72,000
170	5	8	Classik Polished Ebony		76,510
170	5	8	Classik Polished Mahogany/Walnut		87,994
170	5	8	Classik Polished White with bench		81,885
190	6	4	Satin Ebony		70,689
190	6	4	Polished Ebony		75,147
190	6	4	Satin Mahogany/Walnut/Cherry		74,779
190	6	4	Polished Mahogany/Walnut		79,001
190	6	4	Polished White with bench		80,495
190	6	4	Classik Polished Ebony		84,874
190	6	4	Classik Polished Mahogany/Walnut		99,557
190	6	4	Classik Polished White with bench		90,328
190	6	4	Rokoko Polished White with bench		231,056
215	7	2	Polished Ebony		90,223
215	7	2	Polished White with bench		100,632
275	9	1	Polished Ebony		163,272

GEYER, A.

Verticals

Model	Feet	Inches	Description	MSRP	SMP
GU 115		45	Polished Ebony	6,185	4,990
GU 115		45	Polished Mahogany/Walnut	6,685	5,290
GU 115		45	Polished White	6,485	5,190
GU 123		47	Polished Ebony	6,785	5,390
GU 123		47	Polished Mahogany/Walnut	7,235	5,690

Model	Feet	Inches	Description	MSRP	SMP

GEYER, A. *(continued)*

Model	Feet	Inches	Description	MSRP	SMP
GU 123		47	Polished White	7,085	5,590
GU 133		52	Polished Ebony	7,685	5,990
GU 133		52	Polished Mahogany/Walnut	8,285	6,390
GU 133		52	Polished White	7,985	6,190
Grands					
GG 150	4	11	Polished Ebony	12,785	9,590
GG 150	4	11	Polished Mahogany/Walnut	13,685	9,990
GG 150	4	11	Polished White	13,235	9,870
GG 160	5	3	Polished Ebony	14,535	10,590
GG 160	5	3	Polished Mahogany/Walnut	15,285	10,990
GG 160	5	3	Polished White	15,035	10,890
GG 170	5	7	Polished Ebony	16,385	11,790
GG 170	5	7	Polished Mahogany/Walnut	16,715	12,010
GG 170	5	7	Polished White	16,835	12,090
GG 185	6	1	Polished Ebony	18,785	13,390
GG 185	6	1	Polished Mahogany/Walnut	19,585	13,990
GG 185	6	1	Polished White	19,385	13,790
GG 230	7	7	Polished Ebony	29,225	25,990

GROTRIAN

Grotrian Verticals

Model	Feet	Inches	Description	MSRP	SMP
Studio 110		43.5	Satin Ebony	16,373	15,691
Studio 110		43.5	Satin White	16,675	15,980
Friedrich Grotrian		43.5	Polished Ebony	17,119	16,406
Friedrich Grotrian		43.5	Open-pore Walnut	17,119	16,406
Cristal		44	Continental Satin Ebony	22,087	21,167
Cristal		44	Continental Polished Ebony	23,066	22,105
Cristal		44	Continental Open-pore Walnut	23,066	22,105
Cristal		44	Continental Polished Walnut/White	25,272	24,219
Contour		45	Polished Ebony	24,782	23,750
Contour		45	Open-pore Walnut	24,782	23,750
Contour		45	Polished Walnut/White	27,150	26,018
Canto		45	Satin Ebony	24,618	23,593
Canto		45	Polished Ebony	25,762	24,688
Canto		45	Open-pore Walnut	25,762	24,688
Carat		45.5	Polished Ebony	29,028	27,819
Carat		45.5	Open-pore Walnut	29,028	27,819
Carat		45.5	Polished Walnut/White	31,562	30,247
College		48	Satin Ebony	31,378	30,070
College		48	Polished Ebony	33,013	31,639
College		48	Open-pore Walnut	33,013	31,639
Classic		49	Polished Ebony	39,220	37,587
Classic		49	Open-pore Walnut	39,220	37,587
Classic		49	Polished Walnut/White	42,241	40,480

Model	Feet	Inches	Description	MSRP	SMP
GROTRIAN *(continued)*					
Concertino		52	Polished Ebony	49,386	47,329
Concertino		52	Open-pore Walnut	49,386	47,329
Verticals			Chippendale/Rococo/Empire, add	1,411	1,352
Verticals			Sostenuto, add	1,699	1,628

Wilhelm Grotrian Verticals

Model	Feet	Inches	Description	MSRP	SMP
WG-18		47	Polished Ebony	12,999	9,998
WG-23		49	Polished Ebony	14,999	11,198
WG-26		50	Polished Ebony	16,999	12,198
WG-32		52	Polished Ebony	19,999	13,798

Wilhelm Grotrian Studio Verticals

Model	Feet	Inches	Description	MSRP	SMP
WGS-116		46	Polished Ebony	8,599	6,798
WGS-120		47	Polished Ebony	9,699	7,598
WGS-122		48	Polished Ebony	11,099	8,398

Grotrian Grands

Model	Feet	Inches	Description	MSRP	SMP
Chambre	5	5	Satin Ebony	72,544	72,544
Chambre	5	5	Polished Ebony	80,058	80,058
Chambre	5	5	Open-pore Walnut	80,058	80,058
Chambre	5	5	Polished Walnut/White	87,736	87,736
Cabinet	6	3	Satin Ebony	84,306	84,306
Cabinet	6	3	Polished Ebony	93,946	93,946
Cabinet	6	3	Studio Lacquer Ebony	65,310	65,310
Cabinet	6	3	Open-pore Walnut	93,946	93,946
Cabinet	6	3	Polished Walnut/White	102,931	102,931
Charis	6	10	Satin Ebony	99,377	99,377
Charis	6	10	Polished Ebony	108,524	108,524
Charis	6	10	Studio Lacquer Ebony	79,764	79,764
Charis	6	10	Open-pore Walnut	108,524	108,524
Concert	7	4	Satin Ebony	118,354	118,354
Concert	7	4	Polished Ebony	134,001	134,001
Concert	7	4	Open-pore Walnut	134,001	134,001
Concert Royal	9	1	Polished Ebony	179,914	179,914
Concert Royal	9	1	Open-pore Walnut	179,914	179,914
Grands			Chippendale/Empire, add	4,896	4,896
Grands			CS Style, add	5,472	5,472
Grands			Rococo, add	16,416	16,416

Wilhelm Grotrian Grands

Model	Feet	Inches	Description	MSRP	SMP
WG-170	5	7	Polished Ebony	43,099	30,800
WG-188	6	2	Polished Ebony	55,099	38,980
WG-211	6	11	Polished Ebony	80,099	56,980

Wilhelm Grotrian Studio Grands

Model	Feet	Inches	Description	MSRP	SMP
WGS-152	5	1	Polished Ebony	22,999	16,398
WGS-165	5	5	Polished Ebony	26,999	19,398

Model	Feet	Inches	Description	MSRP	SMP

HAESSLER

Prices do not include bench.

Verticals

Model	Feet	Inches	Description	MSRP	SMP
H 118		47	Polished Ebony	25,256	23,753
H 118		47	Satin Mahogany/Walnut	26,429	24,810
H 118		47	Polished Mahogany/Walnut	30,654	28,616
H 118		47	Satin Cherry	26,868	25,205
H 118		47	Polished Cherry	31,123	29,039
H 118		47	Satin Oak/Beech	25,067	23,583
H 118		47	Polished White	27,602	25,867
H 118		47	Polished Bubinga	31,358	29,250
H 118		47	Satin Mahogany w/Vavona Inlay	28,306	26,501
H 118		47	Polished Mahogany w/Vavona Inlay	32,062	29,885
H 118		47	Polished Burl Walnut	31,827	29,673
H 118		47	Satin Burl Walnut w/Walnut Inlay	28,306	26,501
H 118		47	Polished Burl Walnut w/Walnut Inlay	32,062	29,885
H 118		47	Satin Cherry and Yew	28,400	26,586
H 118		47	Polished Cherry and Yew	32,062	29,885
H 124		49	Polished Ebony	27,602	25,867
H 124		49	Satin Mahogany/Walnut	28,635	26,797
H 124		49	Polished Mahogany/Walnut	33,000	30,730
H 124		49	Satin Cherry	28,775	26,923
H 124		49	Polished Cherry	33,470	31,153
H 124		49	Satin Oak/Beech	28,541	26,713
H 124		49	Polished White	29,949	27,981
H 124		49	Polished Bubinga	33,705	31,365
H 124		49	Polished Pyramid Mahogany	37,320	34,622
H 124		49	Satin Mahogany w/Vavona Inlay	30,184	28,193
H 124		49	Polished Mahogany w/Vavona Inlay	35,583	33,057
H 124		49	Polished Burl Walnut	36,850	34,198
H 124		49	Satin Burl Walnut w/Walnut Inlay	30,184	28,193
H 124		49	Polished Burl Walnut w/Walnut Inlay	35,583	33,057
H 124		49	Satin Cherry and Yew	30,184	28,193
H 124		49	Polished Cherry and Yew	36,850	34,198
K 124		49	Polished Ebony	29,856	27,897
K 124		49	Satin Mahogany/Walnut	30,888	28,827
K 124		49	Polished Mahogany/Walnut	35,255	32,761
K 124		49	Satin Cherry	31,030	28,955
K 124		49	Polished Cherry	35,724	33,184
K 124		49	Satin Oak/Beech	30,795	28,743
K 124		49	Polished White	32,266	30,068
K 124		49	Polished Bubinga	35,959	33,395
K 124		49	Polished Pyramid Mahogany	39,573	36,651
K 124		49	Satin Mahogany w/Vavona Inlay	32,438	30,223
K 124		49	Polished Mahogany w/Vavona Inlay	37,836	35,086
K 124		49	Polished Burl Walnut	39,104	36,229

Model	Feet	Inches	Description	MSRP	SMP
HAESSLER *(continued)*					
K 124		49	Satin Burl Walnut w/Walnut Inlay	32,438	30,223
K 124		49	Polished Burl Walnut w/Walnut Inlay	37,836	35,086
K 124		49	Satin Cherry and Yew	32,438	30,223
K 124		49	Polished Cherry and Yew	39,104	36,229
H 132		52	Polished Ebony	30,888	28,827
H 132		52	Satin Mahogany/Walnut	31,358	29,250
H 132		52	Polished Mahogany/Walnut	36,052	33,479
H 132		52	Satin Cherry	32,766	30,519
H 132		52	Polished Cherry	36,522	33,903
H 132		52	Polished White	33,235	30,941
H 132		52	Polished Bubinga	36,991	34,325
H 132		52	Palisander Rosewood	39,104	36,229
H 132		52	Polished Pyramid Mahogany	40,042	37,074
H 132		52	Satin Mahogany w/Vavona Inlay	34,409	31,999
H 132		52	Polished Mahogany w/Vavona Inlay	39,104	36,229
H 132		52	Polished Burl Walnut	40,104	37,130
H 132		52	Satin Burl Walnut w/Walnut Inlay	34,409	31,999
H 132		52	Polished Burl Walnut w/Walnut Inlay	39,104	36,229
H 132		52	Satin Cherry and Yew	34,409	31,999
H 132		52	Polished Cherry and Yew	40,104	37,130
K 132		52	Polished Ebony	34,034	31,661
K 132		52	Satin Mahogany/Walnut	34,504	32,085
K 132		52	Polished Mahogany/Walnut	39,198	36,314
K 132		52	Satin Cherry	35,912	33,353
K 132		52	Polished Cherry	39,668	36,737
K 132		52	Polished White	36,381	33,776
K 132		52	Polished Bubinga	40,137	37,159
K 132		52	Palisander Rosewood	42,249	39,062
K 132		52	Polished Pyramid Mahogany	43,187	39,907
K 132		52	Satin Mahogany w/Vavona Inlay	37,555	34,833
K 132		52	Polished Mahogany w/Vavona Inlay	42,249	39,062
K 132		52	Polished Burl Walnut	42,249	39,062
K 132		52	Satin Burl Walnut w/Walnut Inlay	37,555	34,833
K 132		52	Polished Burl Walnut w/Walnut Inlay	42,249	39,062
K 132		52	Satin Cherry and Yew	37,555	34,833
K 132		52	Polished Cherry and Yew	42,249	39,062
Grands					
H 175	5	8	Polished Ebony	80,195	73,248
H 175	5	8	Satin Mahogany/Walnut	86,210	78,667
H 175	5	8	Polished Mahogany/Walnut	94,310	85,964
H 175	5	8	Satin Cherry	85,488	78,016
H 175	5	8	Polished Cherry	96,516	87,951
H 175	5	8	Polished White	85,809	78,305
H 175	5	8	Polished Bubinga	98,281	89,541
H 175	5	8	Palisander Rosewood	103,133	93,913

Model	Feet	Inches	Description	MSRP	SMP
HAESSLER *(continued)*					
H 175	5	8	Polished Pyramid Mahogany	107,985	98,284
H 175	5	8	Polished Mahogany w/Vavona Inlay	118,131	107,424
H 175	5	8	Polished Burl Walnut	105,338	95,899
H 175	5	8	Polished Burl Walnut w/Walnut Inlay	118,131	107,424
H 175	5	8	Satin Cherry and Yew	111,955	101,860
H 175	5	8	Polished Cherry and Yew	118,131	107,424
H 175	5	8	Classic Alexandra Polished Ebony	95,413	86,958
H 175	5	8	Classic Alexandra Polished Walnut	109,122	99,308
H 175	5	8	Classic Alexandra Burl Walnut	120,042	109,146
H 175	5	8	Classic Alexandra Palisander	117,858	107,178
H 175	5	8	Louis XIV Satin White w/Gold	152,892	138,741
H 175	5	8	Satin and Polished Louis XV Mahogany	116,984	106,391
H 175	5	8	Ambassador Palisander	144,155	130,869
H 175	5	8	Ambassador Walnut	139,786	126,933
H 186	6	1	Polished Ebony	85,047	77,619
H 186	6	1	Satin Mahogany/Walnut	91,426	83,366
H 186	6	1	Polished Mahogany/Walnut	99,162	90,335
H 186	6	1	Satin Cherry	90,340	82,387
H 186	6	1	Polished Cherry	101,368	92,323
H 186	6	1	Polished White	91,000	82,982
H 186	6	1	Polished Bubinga	105,780	96,297
H 186	6	1	Palisander Rosewood	107,985	98,284
H 186	6	1	Polished Pyramid Mahogany	114,602	104,245
H 186	6	1	Polished Mahogany w/Vavona Inlay	122,984	111,796
H 186	6	1	Polished Burl Walnut	110,190	100,270
H 186	6	1	Polished Burl Walnut w/Walnut Inlay	122,984	111,796
H 186	6	1	Satin Cherry and Yew	107,103	97,489
H 186	6	1	Polished Cherry and Yew	122,984	111,796
H 186	6	1	Classic Alexandra Polished Ebony	99,978	91,070
H 186	6	1	Classic Alexandra Polished Walnut	113,926	103,636
H 186	6	1	Classic Alexandra Burl Walnut	124,847	113,475
H 186	6	1	Classic Alexandra Palisander	122,663	111,507
H 186	6	1	Louis XIV Satin White w/Gold	157,260	142,676
H 186	6	1	Satin and Polished Louis XV Mahogany	121,789	110,720
H 186	6	1	Ambassador Palisander	157,260	142,676
H 186	6	1	Ambassador Walnut	152,892	138,741
H 210	6	10	Polished Ebony	99,030	90,216
H 210	6	10	Satin Mahogany/Walnut	106,458	96,908
H 210	6	10	Polished Mahogany/Walnut	117,160	106,550
H 210	6	10	Satin Cherry	107,632	97,966
H 210	6	10	Polished Cherry	119,012	108,218
H 210	6	10	Polished White	105,962	96,461
H 210	6	10	Polished Bubinga	120,778	109,809
H 210	6	10	Palisander Rosewood	130,040	118,153
H 210	6	10	Polished Pyramid Mahogany	136,658	124,115

Model	Feet	Inches	Description	MSRP	SMP
HAESSLER *(continued)*					
H 210	6	10	Polished Mahogany w/Vavona Inlay	145,480	132,063
H 210	6	10	Polished Burl Walnut	127,835	116,167
H 210	6	10	Polished Burl Walnut w/Walnut Inlay	145,480	132,063
H 210	6	10	Satin Cherry and Yew	127,924	116,247
H 210	6	10	Polished Cherry and Yew	145,480	132,063
H 210	6	10	Classic Alexandra Polished Ebony	113,796	103,519
H 210	6	10	Classic Alexandra Polished Walnut	131,749	119,693
H 210	6	10	Classic Alexandra Burl Walnut	142,320	129,216
H 210	6	10	Classic Alexandra Palisander	144,505	131,185
H 210	6	10	Louis XIV Satin White w/Gold	192,207	174,159
H 210	6	10	Satin and Polished Louis XV Mahogany	135,637	123,195
H 210	6	10	Ambassador Palisander	170,365	154,482
H 210	6	10	Ambassador Walnut	165,997	150,547

HAILUN

Verticals

Model	Feet	Inches	Description	MSRP	SMP
HU120		48	Polished Ebony	9,939	7,626
HU121		48	Polished Ebony	10,314	7,876
HU121		48	Polished Mahogany/Walnut	10,692	8,128
HU121		48	Chippendale Polished Mahogany/Walnut	11,157	8,438
HU1-P		48	Polished Ebony	12,885	9,570
HU1-PS		48	Polished Ebony with Nickel Trim	13,368	9,912
HU1-EP		48	Polished Ebony w/mahogany leg, fallboard, cheekblocks	13,857	10,238
HU5-P		50	Polished Ebony	13,935	10,290
HU5-P		50	Polished Ebony with Nickel Trim	14,334	10,556
HU7-P		52	Polished Ebony w/Sostenuto	20,079	14,386

Grands

Model	Feet	Inches	Description	MSRP	SMP
HG150	4	10	Polished Ebony	21,357	15,238
HG151	4	11.5	Polished Ebony	26,520	18,680
HG151	4	11.5	Polished Mahogany/Walnut	27,462	19,308
HG151C	4	11.5	Chippendale Polished Mahogany/Walnut	27,882	19,588
HG161	5	4	Polished Ebony	29,882	20,928
HG161	5	4	Polished Mahogany/Walnut	30,762	21,508
HG161G	5	4	Georgian Polished Mahogany/Walnut	32,304	22,536
HG178	5	10	Polished Ebony	35,493	24,662
HG178	5	10	Polished Mahogany/Walnut	37,170	25,780
HG178B	5	10	Baroque Polished Ebony w/Birds-Eye Maple Accents	37,545	26,030
HG198	6	5	Emerson Polished Ebony	53,505	36,670
HG198	6	5	Emerson Polished Mahogany/Walnut	54,918	37,612
HG218	7	2	Paulello Polished Ebony	72,882	49,588

Model	Feet	Inches	Description	MSRP	SMP

HALLET, DAVIS & CO.

Heritage Collection Verticals

Model	Feet	Inches	Description	MSRP	SMP
H108		43	Continental Polished Ebony	5,295	4,300
H117H		46	Polished Ebony	5,950	4,500
H117H		46	Polished Mahogany	6,150	4,590
H118F		46	Demi-Chippendale Polished Ebony	5,995	4,700
H118F		46	Demi-Chippendale Polished Mahogany	6,195	4,790

Signature Collection Verticals

Model	Feet	Inches	Description	MSRP	SMP
HS109D		43	Continental Polished Ebony	5,895	4,700
HS109D		43	Continental Polished Mahogany	6,195	4,900
HS115M2		45	Classic Studio Polished Ebony	7,395	4,990
HS115M2		45	Classic Studio Polished Mahogany/Walnut/White	7,595	5,190
HS118M		46.5	Polished Ebony	7,795	5,390
HS118M		46.5	Polished Mahogany/Walnut/White	7,995	5,590
HS121S		48	Polished Ebony	8,995	5,790
HS121S		48	Polished Mahogany/Walnut/White	9,295	5,990
HS131Y		52	Polished Ebony	9,895	6,790

Heritage Collection Grands

Model	Feet	Inches	Description	MSRP	SMP
H142C	4	7	Polished Ebony	13,195	9,390

Signature Collection Grands

Model	Feet	Inches	Description	MSRP	SMP
HS148	4	10	Satin Ebony	15,695	10,390
HS148	4	10	Polished Ebony	14,995	9,790
HS148	4	10	Polished Ebony w/Silver Plate	15,695	10,390
HS148	4	10	Polished Mahogany/Walnut/White	15,695	10,390
HS148	4	10	Polished White w/Silver Plate	16,495	10,990
HS160	5	3	Satin Ebony	16,995	11,590
HS160	5	3	Polished Ebony	16,495	10,990
HS160	5	3	Polished Ebony w/Silver Plate	16,995	11,590
HS160	5	3	Polished Mahogany/Walnut/White	16,995	11,590
HS170	5	7	Satin Ebony	17,995	12,790
HS170	5	7	Polished Ebony	17,495	12,190
HS170	5	7	Polished Mahogany/Walnut/White	17,995	12,790
HS188	6	2	Satin Ebony	20,995	15,390
HS188	6	2	Polished Ebony	20,495	14,790
HS188	6	2	Polished Mahogany/Walnut	20,995	15,390
HS212	7		Polished Ebony	29,995	28,990

HARDMAN, PECK & CO.

Performance Series Verticals

Model	Feet	Inches	Description	MSRP	SMP
R110S		44	Polished Ebony	5,495	4,310
R110S		44	Polished Mahogany	5,695	4,390
R115LS		45	Polished Ebony	5,995	4,510
R115LS		45	Polished Mahogany	6,195	4,590

Model	Feet	Inches	Description	MSRP	SMP
HARDMAN, PECK & CO. *(continued)*					
R116		46	School Polished Ebony	6,695	4,990
R116		46	School Satin Cherry	6,895	5,110
R117XK		46	Chippendale Polished Mahogany	6,695	4,910
R120LS		48	Polished Ebony	6,495	4,910
R120LS		48	Polished Mahogany	6,695	4,990
R132HA		52	Polished Ebony	9,495	6,490
Concert Series Verticals					
R110C		44	Polished Ebony	5,795	4,590
R110C		44	Polished Mahogany	5,995	4,790
R115GC		45	Polished Ebony	6,595	4,790
R115GC		45	Polished Mahogany	6,995	4,990
R123C		49	Polished Ebony	7,295	5,390
R123C		49	Polished Mahogany	7,595	5,590
Performance Series Grands					
R143S	4	8	Polished Mahogany	14,995	9,790
R143F	4	8	French Provincial Polished Mahogany	15,395	10,190
R150S	5		Polished Ebony	15,995	9,990
R158S	5	3	Polished Ebony	16,795	10,590
R158S	5	3	Polished Mahogany	17,495	10,990
R168S	5	7	Polished Ebony	18,195	11,390
R168S	5	7	Polished Mahogany	18,995	11,790
R185S	6	1	Polished Ebony	20,995	13,190
R185S	6	1	Polished Mahogany	22,395	13,790
Concert Series Grands					
R146C	4	10	Polished Ebony	14,595	9,390
R146C	4	10	Polished Mahogany	15,395	9,990
R165C	5	5	Polished Ebony	18,495	11,390
R165C	5	5	Polished Mahogany	19,495	11,990

HEINTZMAN & CO.

Heintzman Verticals

Model	Feet	Inches	Description	MSRP	SMP
121DL		48	Satin Mahogany	7,995	7,380
123B		48.5	Polished Mahogany	8,795	7,580
123F		48.5	French Provincial Polished Mahogany	7,995	6,980
126C		50	Polished Ebony	8,795	7,600
126 Royal		50	Polished Ebony	9,795	8,200
132D		52	Polished Mahogany, Decorative Panel	11,795	8,980
132E		52	French Provincial Polished Ebony	11,795	8,780
132E		52	French Provincial Satin and Polished Mahogany	11,795	8,980
132 Royal		52	Satin Mahogany	12,795	9,580
140CK		55	Polished Mahogany	14,995	10,980

Model	Feet	Inches	Description	MSRP	SMP

HEINTZMAN & CO. *(continued)*
Gerhard Heintzman Verticals

Model	Feet	Inches	Description	MSRP	SMP
G118		47	Polished Ebony w/Silver Plate and Trim	4,995	4,995
G118		47	Polished Mahogany w/Silver Plate and Trim	5,195	5,195
G120		48	Polished Ebony w/Silver Plate and Trim	5,995	5,700
G120		48	Polished Mahogany w/Silver Plate and Trim	6,195	5,900
G126		50	Polished Ebony w/Silver Plate and Trim	7,995	6,400
G126		50	Polished Mahogany w/Silver Plate and Trim	8,195	6,600
G132		52	Polished Ebony w/Silver Plate and Trim	9,295	7,200

Heintzman Grands

Model	Feet	Inches	Description	MSRP	SMP
168	5	6	Polished Ebony	18,995	16,990
168	5	6	Polished Mahogany	19,995	17,390
168 Royal	5	6	Polished Ebony	23,995	17,990
186	6	1	Polished Ebony	21,995	18,980
186	6	1	Polished Mahogany	22,995	20,180
186 Royal	6	1	Polished Ebony	26,995	19,980
203	6	8	Polished Ebony	24,995	20,580
203 Royal	6	8	Polished Ebony	29,995	21,580
277	9		Polished Ebony	89,995	60,995

Gerhard Heintzman Grands

Model	Feet	Inches	Description	MSRP	SMP
G152	5		Polished Ebony	9,995	9,995
G152	5		Polished White	11,995	11,995
G152R	5		Empire Polished Mahogany	11,995	11,995
G168	5	6	Polished Ebony	15,995	12,800
G168	5	6	Polished White	19,995	13,800
G168R	5	6	Empire Polished Mahogany	17,995	13,800

HOFFMANN, W.
Vision Series Verticals

Model	Feet	Inches	Description	MSRP	SMP
V112		44.5	Polished Ebony	12,500	12,142
V112		44.5	Polished Mahogany/Walnut	15,900	15,044
V112		44.5	Polished White	14,900	13,593
V112		44.5	Chippendale Polished Mahogany	16,500	16,205
V112		44.5	Chippendale Polished Walnut	16,500	16,205
V120		47.6	Polished Ebony	13,500	12,868
V120		47.6	Polished Mahogany/Walnut	16,500	16,044
V120		47.6	Polished White	15,500	15,044
V120		47.6	Chippendale Polished Mahogany	17,900	17,656
V120		47.6	Chippendale Polished Walnut	17,900	17,656
V120		47.6	Rococo Satin White	19,900	18,381
V120		47.6	Rococo Satin White w/Gold Painting	19,900	18,381
V126		49.6	Polished Ebony	14,900	14,319
V126		49.6	Polished White	17,900	16,495
V131		51.8	Polished Ebony	16,900	15,770

Model	Feet	Inches	Description	MSRP	SMP

HOFFMANN, W. *(continued)*

Tradition Series Verticals

Model	Feet	Inches	Description	MSRP	SMP
T122		48	Polished Ebony	16,900	16,044
T122		48	Satin Mahogany/Walnut	19,900	19,672
T122		48	Polished Mahogany/Walnut	19,900	19,672
T122		48	Polished White	18,900	18,221
T128		50.4	Polished Ebony	17,900	17,495
T128		50.4	Satin Mahogany/Walnut	21,900	21,123
T128		50.4	Polished Mahogany/Walnut	21,900	21,123
T128		50.4	Polished White	20,900	19,672

Professional Series Verticals

Model	Feet	Inches	Description	MSRP	SMP
P114		45	Polished Ebony w/Chrome Hardware	17,900	17,495
P114		45	Polished White w/Chrome Hardware	19,900	19,672
P120		47.2	Polished Ebony w/Chrome Hardware	18,900	18,801
P120		47.2	Polished White w/Chrome Hardware	20,900	20,793
P126		49.6	Polished Ebony w/Chrome Hardware	20,500	20,397

Vision Series Grands

Model	Feet	Inches	Description	MSRP	SMP
V158	5	2	Polished Ebony	29,900	29,247
V158	5	2	Polished Mahogany/Walnut	34,900	33,600
V158	5	2	Polished White	33,900	33,149
V175	5	9	Polished Ebony	32,900	32,423
V175	5	9	Polished Walnut/Mahogany	37,900	36,776
V175	5	9	Polished White	36,900	36,325
V183	6		Polished Ebony	35,900	35,325
V183	6		Polished Walnut/Mahogany	40,900	39,678
V183	6		Polished White	39,900	39,227

Tradition Series Grands

Model	Feet	Inches	Description	MSRP	SMP
T161	5	3	Polished Ebony	41,900	41,885
T161	5	3	Polished Mahogany/Walnut	47,900	46,870
T161	5	3	Polished White	46,900	46,313
T177	5	10	Polished Ebony	47,900	45,313
T177	5	10	Polished Mahogany/Walnut	52,900	49,983
T177	5	10	Polished White	51,900	49,426
T186	6	1	Polished Ebony	52,900	51,539
T186	6	1	Polished Mahogany/Walnut	57,900	56,209
T186	6	1	Polished White	56,900	55,652

Professional Series Grands

Model	Feet	Inches	Description	MSRP	SMP
P162	5	4	Polished Ebony w/Chrome Hardware	52,900	50,916
P188	6	2	Polished Ebony w/Chrome Hardware	57,900	55,586
P206	6	9	Polished Ebony w/Chrome Hardware	64,900	61,812

Model	Feet	Inches	Description	MSRP	SMP
HUPFELD					
Studio Edition Verticals					
P112		44	Polished Ebony	6,475	6,475
P118		47	Polished Ebony	6,740	6,712
P118		47	Polished White	6,880	6,831
P125		49	Polished Ebony	8,226	7,971
Europe Edition Verticals					
P116E		46	Polished Ebony	9,599	9,532
P116E		46	Satin Mahogany/Walnut	10,498	10,332
P116E		46	Satin Cherry	11,403	11,136
P116E		46	Polished Mahogany/Walnut	10,198	10,065
P116E		46	Polished Cherry/White	11,403	11,136
P122E		48	Polished Ebony	10,650	10,467
P122E		48	Satin Mahogany/Walnut	11,950	11,622
P122E		48	Satin Cherry	12,457	12,073
P122E		48	Polished Mahogany/Walnut	11,252	11,002
P122E		48	Polished Cherry	12,150	11,800
P122E		48	Polished Bubinga	13,330	12,849
P122E		48	Polished White	12,457	12,073
P132E		52	Polished Ebony	11,282	11,028
P132E		52	Satin Mahogany/Walnut	12,595	12,196
P132E		52	Satin Cherry	14,206	13,628
P132E		52	Polished Mahogany/Walnut	11,885	11,564
P132E		52	Polished Cherry/White	13,089	12,635
P132E		52	Polished Bubinga	15,740	14,991
Studio Edition Grands					
F 148	4	10	Polished Ebony	18,029	17,026
F 148	4	10	Polished Mahogany/Walnut	19,079	17,959
F 148	4	10	Polished White	18,279	17,248
F 160	5	3	Polished Ebony	20,829	19,515
F 160	5	3	Polished Mahogany/Walnut	21,689	20,279
F 160	5	3	Polished White	21,531	20,139
F 188	6	2	Polished Ebony	29,756	27,450
F 188	6	2	Polished Mahogany/Walnut	30,370	27,996
F 188	6	2	Polished White	30,458	28,074
F 213	7		Polished Ebony	34,409	31,586
F 213	7		Polished White	38,391	35,125
Europe Edition Grands					
F 160E	5	3	Polished Ebony	32,919	30,261
F 160E	5	3	Polished Mahogany/Walnut	35,585	32,631
F 160E	5	3	Polished Cherry/Bubinga/White	38,345	35,084
F 175E	5	9	Polished Ebony	36,374	33,332
F 175E	5	9	Polished Mahogany/Walnut	45,838	41,745

PIANOBUYER *Model & Price Supplement*

Model	Feet	Inches	Description	MSRP	SMP
HUPFELD *(continued)*					
F 175E	5	9	Polished Bubinga/White	48,598	44,198
F 190E	6	3	Polished Ebony	43,472	39,642
F 190E	6	3	Polished Mahogany/Walnut	45,838	41,745
F 190E	6	3	Polished Bubinga/White	48,598	44,198
F 210E	6	11	Polished Ebony	48,598	44,198
F 230E	7	7	Polished Ebony	56,484	51,208

IRMLER

Studio Edition Verticals

Model	Inches	Description	MSRP	SMP
P112	44	Polished Ebony	6,475	6,475
P118	47	Polished Ebony	6,740	6,712
P118	47	Polished White	6,880	6,831
P125	49	Polished Ebony	8,226	7,971

Art Design Verticals

Model	Inches	Description	MSRP	SMP
Da Vinci	48	Polished Ebony w/Verone Veneer Liner	9,531	9,077
Gina	49	Polished Ebony	10,514	9,910
Monique	49	Polished Ebony	11,480	10,729
Louis	49	Polished Ebony	11,127	10,430
Titus	49	Polished Ebony	11,480	10,729
Alexa	49	Polished Ebony	13,087	12,091
Carlo	49	Polished Ebony	13,414	12,368
Monet	49	Polished Ebony w/Verone Veneer Inner Fallboard & Lid	10,065	9,530
Van Gogh	51	Polished Ebony w/Vavone Front Liner Panels & Legs	12,738	11,795

Supreme Edition Verticals

Model	Inches	Description	MSRP	SMP
SP118	47	Polished Ebony	8,373	8,096
SP121	48	Polished Ebony	8,943	8,579
SP125	49	Polished Ebony	9,818	9,320
SP132	52	Polished Ebony	10,888	10,227

Professional Edition Verticals

Model	Inches	Description	MSRP	SMP
P116E	46	Polished Ebony	9,599	9,135
P116E	46	Satin Mahogany/Walnut	10,498	9,897
P116E	46	Satin Cherry	11,403	10,664
P116E	46	Polished Mahogany/Walnut	10,198	9,642
P116E	46	Polished Cherry/White	11,403	10,664
P122E	48	Polished Ebony	10,650	10,025
P122E	48	Satin Mahogany/Walnut	11,950	11,127
P122E	48	Satin Cherry	12,457	11,557
P122E	48	Polished Mahogany/Walnut	11,252	10,536
P122E	48	Polished Cherry	12,150	11,297
P122E	48	Polished Bubinga	13,330	12,297
P122E	48	Polished White	12,457	11,557
P132E	52	Polished Ebony	11,282	10,561

Model	Feet	Inches	Description	MSRP	SMP

IRMLER *(continued)*

Model	Feet	Inches	Description	MSRP	SMP
P132E		52	Satin Mahogany/Walnut	12,595	11,674
P132E		52	Satin Cherry	14,206	13,039
P132E		52	Polished Mahogany/Walnut	11,885	11,072
P132E		52	Polished Cherry/White	13,089	12,092
P132E		52	Polished Bubinga	15,740	14,339

Studio Edition Grands

Model	Feet	Inches	Description	MSRP	SMP
F148	4	10	Polished Ebony	18,029	16,279
F148	4	10	Polished Mahogany/Walnut	19,079	17,169
F148	4	10	Polished White	18,279	16,491
F160	5	3	Polished Ebony	20,829	18,652
F160	5	3	Polished Mahogany/Walnut	21,689	19,381
F160	5	3	Polished White	21,531	19,247
F188	6	2	Polished Ebony	29,756	26,217
F188	6	2	Polished Mahogany/Walnut	30,370	26,737
F188	6	2	Polished White	30,458	26,812
F213	7		Polished Ebony	36,409	31,855
F213	7		Polished White	38,391	33,535

Professional Edition Grands

Model	Feet	Inches	Description	MSRP	SMP
F160E	5	3	Polished Ebony	32,919	28,897
F160E	5	3	Polished Mahogany/Walnut	35,585	31,157
F160E	5	3	Polished Cherry	38,345	33,496
F160E	5	3	Polished White	38,345	33,496
F160E	5	3	Polished Bubinga	38,345	33,496
F175E	5	9	Polished Ebony	36,374	31,825
F175E	5	9	Polished Mahogany/Walnut	38,740	33,831
F175E	5	9	Polished White	41,500	36,169
F175E	5	9	Polished Bubinga	41,500	36,169
F190E	6	3	Polished Ebony	43,472	37,841
F190E	6	3	Polished Mahogany/Walnut	45,838	39,846
F190E	6	3	Polished White	48,598	42,185
F190E	6	3	Polished Bubinga	48,598	42,185
F210E	6	10.5	Polished Ebony	48,598	42,185
F230E	7	6.5	Polished Ebony	56,484	48,868

KAWAI

Verticals

Model	Feet	Inches	Description	MSRP	SMP
K-15		44	Continental Polished Ebony	5,895	5,690
K-15		44	Continental Polished Mahogany	6,095	5,890
K-15		44	Continental Polished Snow White	6,195	5,990
506N		44.5	Satin Ebony/Mahogany	5,895	5,690
508		44.5	Satin Mahogany	6,695	6,390
607		44.5	French Renaissance Satin Cherry	7,995	7,390
607		44.5	Queen Anne Satin Mahogany	7,995	7,390

Model	Feet	Inches	Description	MSRP	SMP

KAWAI (*continued*)

Model	Feet	Inches	Description	MSRP	SMP
K-200		45	Satin and Polished Ebony	7,995	7,390
K-200		45	Satin and Polished Mahogany	8,695	7,990
K-200NKL		45	Satin and Polished Ebony with Nickel Trim	8,395	7,690
ST-1		46	Satin Ebony/Oak/Walnut/Cherry	8,695	7,990
ST-1		46	Polished Ebony	9,295	8,590
K-300		48	Satin and Polished Ebony	12,095	10,790
K-300		48	Satin and Polished Mahogany	12,895	11,290
K-300		48	Polished Snow White	13,095	11,490
K-300NKL		48	Satin and Polished Ebony with Nickel Trim	12,495	10,990
K-400		48	Polished Ebony	12,895	11,290
K-400NKL		48	Polished Ebony with Nickel Trim	13,195	11,590
K-500		51	Satin and Polished Ebony	15,695	13,590
K-500		51	Polished Sapele Mahogany	17,695	15,190
K-800		53	Polished Ebony	24,995	20,990

AnyTime (Silent) Verticals

Model	Feet	Inches	Description	MSRP	SMP
K-200 ATX3-CA		45	AnyTime Polished Ebony w/CA Sound	12,495	10,990
K-300 AURES		48	AnyTime Polished Ebony w/Soundboard Speaker	17,495	14,990

Grands

Model	Feet	Inches	Description	MSRP	SMP
GL-10	5		Satin and Polished Ebony	16,295	15,190
GL-10	5		Polished Ebony with Nickel Trim	17,195	15,990
GL-10	5		Polished Mahogany/Snow White	17,895	16,590
GL-10	5		French Provincial Polished Mahogany	18,995	17,590
GL-20	5	2	Satin and Polished Ebony	19,095	17,590
GL-20	5	2	Polished Mahogany	21,395	19,590
GL-20	5	2	Polished Snow White	21,395	19,590
GL-30	5	5	Satin and Polished Ebony	29,295	26,790
GL-30	5	5	Polished Sapele Mahogany	35,195	31,990
GL-30	5	5	Satin Dark Walnut	35,195	31,990
GL-30	5	5	Polished Snow White	33,995	30,790
GX-1 BLK	5	5	Satin and Polished Ebony	39,495	32,590
GX-1 BLK	5	5	Polished Dark Walnut	44,795	36,790
GL-40	5	11	Satin and Polished Ebony	34,495	31,390
GL-40	5	11	Polished Sapele Mahogany	40,895	36,990
GL-40	5	11	Satin Dark Walnut	40,895	36,990
GX-2 BLK	5	11	Satin and Polished Ebony	45,495	37,390
GX-2 BLK	5	11	Satin Walnut/Cherry/Oak	50,495	41,390
GX-2 BLK	5	11	Polished Walnut/Sapeli Mahogany	52,495	42,990
GX-2 BLK	5	11	Polished Snow White	48,495	39,790
GL-50	6	2	Polished Ebony	39,795	35,990
GX-3 BLK	6	2	Satin and Polished Ebony	58,495	47,790
GX-5 BLK	6	7	Satin and Polished Ebony	66,195	53,990
GX-6 BLK	7		Satin and Polished Ebony	74,195	60,390
GX-7 BLK	7	6	Satin and Polished Ebony	85,195	69,790
EX-L	9	1	Polished Ebony	234,695	188,790
EX-L	9	1	Polished Ebony	234,695	188,790

Model	Feet	Inches	Description	MSRP	SMP
KAWAI *(continued)*					
AnyTime (Silent) Grands					
GL-30 ATX2-SS	5	5	AnyTime Polished Ebony w/Soundboard Speaker	32,295	29,390

KAWAI, SHIGERU

Grands

Model	Feet	Inches	Description	MSRP	SMP
SK-2	5	11	Polished Ebony	68,495	55,800
SK-2	5	11	Polished Sapele Mahogany	78,995	64,200
SK-3	6	2	Polished Ebony	79,995	65,000
SK-3	6	2	Polished Sapele Mahogany	91,995	74,600
SK-3	6	2	Polished Pyramid Mahogany	106,495	86,200
SK-5	6	7	Polished Ebony	92,295	74,800
SK-6	7		Polished Ebony	103,995	84,200
SK-7	7	6	Polished Ebony	115,295	93,200
SK-EX	9	1	Polished Ebony	256,495	206,200

KAYSERBURG

Verticals

Model	Feet	Inches	Description	MSRP	SMP
KA1		48	Polished Ebony	15,995	12,990
KA1		48	Polished Walnut	16,795	13,590
KA2		49	Polished Ebony	16,995	13,595
KA2		49	Polished Walnut	17,795	14,235
KA3		50	Polished Ebony	18,495	14,795
KA3		50	Polished Walnut	19,995	15,995
KA5		51	Polished Ebony	20,995	16,190
KA6		52	Polished Ebony	21,495	16,495

Grands

Model	Feet	Inches	Description	MSRP	SMP
KA151	5		Polished Ebony	38,995	31,195
KA160	5	3	Polished Ebony	47,995	38,395
KA180	5	9	Polished Ebony	59,995	52,990

KINGSBURG

Verticals

Model	Feet	Inches	Description	MSRP	SMP
LM 116		46	Chippendale Polished Walnut	6,610	5,893
KG 120		48	Polished Ebony	9,459	7,326
KU 120		48	Polished Ebony	8,815	6,114
KU 120		48	Satin and Polished Mahogany/Walnut	9,146	6,334
KG 122		48	Polished Ebony	10,085	7,657
KF 122		48	Polished Ebony	13,473	9,440
KF 123		50	Polished White & Red	13,480	9,862
KG 123		50	Decorator Satin Walnut	12,402	9,321
KU 123		50	Decorator Satin Walnut	9,917	6,996

Model	Feet	Inches	Description	MSRP	SMP

KINGSBURG *(continued)*

Model	Feet	Inches	Description	MSRP	SMP
KG 125		50	Polished Ebony	10,367	7,998
KU 125		50	Polished Ebony	9,917	6,775
KU 125		50	Polished Ebony w/Inlay	10,602	7,216
KU 125		50	Satin and Polished Mahogany/Walnut	10,469	6,996
KF 126		50	Satin Walnut	14,720	10,744
KF 128		50	Polished Ebony	14,498	11,626
KF 133		52	Polished Ebony	16,483	12,508
KG 133		52	Polished Ebony	12,497	9,421
KU 133		52	Polished Ebony	10,574	7,437
KU 133		52	Polished Mahogany/Walnut	11,003	7,657

Grands

Model	Feet	Inches	Description	MSRP	SMP
KF 158	5	3	Polished Ebony	25,909	25,859
KG 158	5	3	Polished Ebony	19,840	13,611
KG 158	5	3	Polished Ebony w/Inlay	20,942	14,272
KG 158	5	3	Polished Mahogany/Walnut	20,391	14,052
KG 175	5	9	Polished Ebony	22,320	14,006
KF 185	6	1	Polished Ebony	33,020	32,970
KG 185	6	1	Polished Ebony	24,250	15,375
KG 185	6	1	Polished Ebony w/Inlay	25,904	16,036
KG 185	6	1	Polished Mahogany/Walnut	25,352	15,816
KF 228	7	4	Polished Ebony	69,458	64,195

KNABE, WM.

Baltimore Series Verticals

Model	Feet	Inches	Description	MSRP	SMP
WV 43		43	Continental Polished Ebony	7,519	5,398
WV 243F		43	French Provincial Satin Cherry	8,239	5,798
WV 243T		43	Satin Mahogany/Walnut	8,239	5,798
WV 115		45	Satin Ebony	9,059	6,298
WV 115		45	Polished Ebony	8,239	5,798
WV 118H		46.5	Satin Ebony	9,579	6,598
WV 118H		46.5	Polished Ebony	9,269	6,398

Academy Series Verticals

Model	Feet	Inches	Description	MSRP	SMP
WMV 245		45	Satin Ebony	8,959	6,198
WMV 245		45	Polished Ebony	8,549	5,998
WMV 247		46.5	Satin Ebony/Walnut	10,299	6,998
WMV 247		46.5	Polished Ebony	9,989	6,798
WMV 647F		46.5	French Provincial Satin Cherry	9,989	6,798
WMV 647R		46.5	Renaissance Satin Walnut	9,989	6,798
WMV 647T		46.5	Satin Mahogany	9,989	6,798
WMV 121M		47.5	Satin Ebony	10,299	6,998
WMV 121M		47.5	Polished Ebony	9,989	6,798
WMV 132		52	Satin Ebony	12,669	8,398
WMV 132		52	Polished Ebony	12,049	7,998

Model	Feet	Inches	Description	MSRP	SMP

KNABE, WM. *(continued)*

Concert Artist Series Verticals

Model	Feet	Inches	Description	MSRP	SMP
WKV 118F		47	French Provincial Lacquer Semigloss Cherry	14,419	9,398
WKV 118R		47	Renaissance Lacquer Satin Ebony	14,419	9,398
WKV 118R		47	Renaissance Lacquer Semigloss Walnut	14,419	9,398
WKV 118T		47	Lacquer Semigloss Mahogany	14,419	9,398
WKV 121		48	Satin Ebony	15,039	9,798
WKV 121		48	Polished Ebony	14,419	9,398
WKV 132MD		52	Satin Ebony	16,479	10,598
WKV 132MD		52	Polished Ebony	15,039	9,798

Baltimore Series Grands

Model	Feet	Inches	Description	MSRP	SMP
WG 49	4	9	Satin Ebony	18,179	11,918
WG 49	4	9	Polished Ebony	16,809	11,098
WG 49	4	9	Polished Mahogany/Walnut	18,869	12,318
WG 54	5	4	Satin Ebony	20,599	12,998
WG 54	5	4	Polished Ebony	19,159	12,198
WG 54	5	4	Polished Mahogany/Walnut	20,909	13,198
WG 54	5	4	Polished Ebony w/Bubinga or Pommele Accents	23,999	14,998
WSG 54	5	4	M Leg w/Bubinga or Pommele Accents	27,399	16,998
WG 59	5	9	Satin Ebony	25,439	15,798
WG 59	5	9	Polished Ebony	23,689	14,798
WG 61	6	1	Satin Ebony	26,779	16,598
WG 61	6	1	Polished Ebony	25,439	15,798

Academy Series Grands

Model	Feet	Inches	Description	MSRP	SMP
WMG 610	5	9	Satin Ebony	28,529	17,598
WMG 610	5	9	Polished Ebony	27,089	16,798
WMG 660	6	1	Satin Ebony	31,929	19,598
WMG 660	6	1	Polished Ebony	30,589	18,798
WFM 700T	6	10	Satin Ebony	35,019	21,398
WFM 700T	6	10	Polished Ebony	33,679	20,598

Concert Artist Series Grands

Model	Feet	Inches	Description	MSRP	SMP
WKG 53	5	3	Satin Ebony	34,299	20,998
WKG 53	5	3	Polished Ebony	33,269	20,398
WKG 58	5	8	Satin Ebony	42,229	25,598
WKG 58	5	8	Polished Ebony	41,199	24,998
WKG 70	7		Satin Ebony	57,989	34,798
WKG 70	7		Polished Ebony	56,959	34,198
WKG 76	7	6	Satin Ebony	59,949	35,898
WKG 76	7	6	Polished Ebony	59,019	35,398
WKG 90	9	2	Satin Ebony	152,029	89,598
WKG 90	9	2	Polished Ebony	147,909	87,198

Model	Feet	Inches	Description	MSRP	SMP

KRAUSE BERLIN, ERNST

Verticals

Model	Feet	Inches	Description	MSRP	SMP
KC-123		49	Polished Ebony	10,590	8,790
KC-123		49	Polished Mahogany/Walnut	11,590	9,690
KC-126		50	Polished Ebony	11,590	9,690
KC-126		50	Polished Mahogany/Walnut	12,590	10,490
KC-133		53	Polished Ebony	14,540	12,090

Grands

Model	Feet	Inches	Description	MSRP	SMP
KC-160	5	3	Polished Ebony	29,000	23,990
KC-160	5	3	Polished Mahogany/Walnut	33,200	27,590
KC-170	5	7	Polished Ebony	31,540	26,190
KC-170	5	7	Polished Mahogany/Walnut	34,550	28,690
KC-186	6	1	Polished Ebony	35,750	29,690
KC-186	6	1	Polished Mahogany/Walnut	38,750	32,190

MASON & HAMLIN

Verticals

Model	Feet	Inches	Description	MSRP	SMP
50		50	Satin Ebony	32,226	29,424
50		50	Polished Ebony	30,185	27,624
50		50	Cambridge Collection, Polished Ebony w/Bubinga or Macassar	35,287	30,324

Grands

Model	Feet	Inches	Description	MSRP	SMP
B	5	4	Satin Ebony	78,214	66,153
B	5	4	Polished Ebony	76,173	64,453
B	5	4	Polished Mahogany/Walnut	81,308	68,730
B	5	4	Polished Pyramid Mahogany	98,983	83,453
B	5	4	Polished Rosewood	90,275	76,200
B	5	4	Polished Bubinga	93,479	78,869
B	5	4	Polished Macassar Ebony	98,983	83,453
A	5	8	Satin Ebony	79,438	67,173
A	5	8	Polished Ebony	77,398	65,473
A	5	8	Polished Mahogany/Walnut	82,531	69,750
A	5	8	Polished Pyramid Mahogany	100,208	84,473
A	5	8	Polished Rosewood	91,500	77,220
A	5	8	Polished Bubinga	94,703	79,889
A	5	8	Polished Macassar Ebony	100,208	84,473
AA	6	4	Satin Ebony	90,387	76,293
AA	6	4	Polished Ebony	88,346	74,593
AA	6	4	Polished Mahogany/Walnut	93,118	78,568
AA	6	4	Polished Pyramid Mahogany	106,995	90,128
AA*	6	4	Polished Rosewood	98,265	82,855
AA	6	4	Polished Bubinga	101,462	85,517
AA	6	4	Polished Macassar Ebony	106,995	90,128
BB	7		Satin Ebony	102,293	86,211

MASON & HAMLIN (continued)

Model	Feet	Inches	Description	MSRP	SMP
BB	7		Polished Ebony	100,252	84,511
BB	7		Polished Mahogany/Walnut	103,800	87,465
BB	7		Polished Pyramid Mahogany	123,589	103,950
BB	7		Polished Rosewood	116,197	97,793
BB	7		Polished Bubinga	119,080	100,193
BB	7		Polished Macassar Ebony	123,589	103,950
CC	9	4	Satin Ebony	151,093	126,861
CC	9	4	Polished Ebony	149,053	125,161
CC	9	4	Polished Mahogany/Walnut	159,541	133,898
CC	9	4	Polished Pyramid Mahogany	181,635	152,303
CC	9	4	Polished Rosewood	168,612	141,454
CC	9	4	Polished Bubinga	174,263	146,161
CC	9	4	Polished Macassar Ebony	181,635	152,303
VX	9	4	Satin Ebony	181,706	152,361
VX	9	4	Polished Ebony	179,665	150,661
VX	9	4	Polished Mahogany/Walnut	190,153	159,398
VX	9	4	Polished Pyramid Mahogany	212,248	177,803
VX	9	4	Polished Rosewood	199,224	166,954
VX	9	4	Polished Bubinga	204,875	171,661
VX	9	4	Polished Macassar Ebony	212,248	177,803
Grands			Cambridge Collection, add	8,000	6,800

Artist Series Verticals

Model	Feet	Inches	Description	MSRP	SMP
MHA 123U		48	Polished Ebony	9,895	9,895
MHA 131U		51	Polished Ebony	11,834	11,834

Artist Series Grands

Model	Feet	Inches	Description	MSRP	SMP
MHA 160G	5	3	Polished Ebony	18,265	18,265
MHA 188G	6	2	Polished Ebony	23,346	23,346

Classic Series Verticals

Model	Feet	Inches	Description	MSRP	SMP
MHC 120U		47	Polished Ebony	7,540	7,540

Classic Series Grands

Model	Feet	Inches	Description	MSRP	SMP
MHC 150G	4	11	Polished Ebony	14,977	14,977
MHC 170G	5	6	Polished Ebony	15,908	15,908

PALATINO

Verticals

Model	Feet	Inches	Description	MSRP	SMP
PUP-22C		48	Polished Mahogany/Cherry	5,000	5,000
PUP-22C		48	Satin Walnut	5,000	5,000
PUP-123T		48	Torino Polished Ebony	5,900	5,900
PUP-123T		48	Torino Polished Dark Walnut	6,200	6,200
PUP-125		50	Satin and Polished Ebony	5,950	5,950
PUP-125		50	Polished Mahogany/White	5,950	5,950
PUP-126		50	Capri Polished Ebony	6,900	6,900
PUP-126		50	Capri Polished Dark Walnut	7,500	7,500

Model	Feet	Inches	Description	MSRP	SMP

PALATINO (continued)
Grands

Model	Feet	Inches	Description	MSRP	SMP
PGD-50	5		Milano Polished Ebony	12,000	12,000
PGD-50	5		Milano Polished Dark Walnut	12,500	12,500
PGD-59	5	9	Roma Polished Ebony	13,400	13,400
PGD-62	6	2	Firenze Polished Ebony	15,400	15,400

PEARL RIVER
Verticals

Model	Feet	Inches	Description	MSRP	SMP
UP 109D		43	Continental Polished Ebony	4,795	4,487
UP 109D		43	Continental Polished Mahogany	4,995	4,633
EU 110		43	Polished Ebony	4,950	4,600
EU 110 Silent		43	Polished Ebony w/Silent System	8,195	6,960
EU 111PA		43	French Provincial Satin Cherry	6,095	5,433
EU 111PB		43	Mediterranean Satin Walnut	6,095	5,433
EU 111PC		43	Italian Provincial Satin Mahogany	6,095	5,433
UP 115E		45	Satin Ebony/Mahogany (School)	7,995	6,815
UP 115M5		45	Polished Ebony	5,095	4,705
UP 115M5		45	Polished Mahogany/Walnut/White	5,295	4,851
EU 118S		47	Polished Ebony w/Silver Hardware	5,595	5,069
EU 118S		47	Polished Mahogany/Walnut w/Silver Hardware	6,095	5,433
PE 121		48	Two-Tone Polished Ebony w/Sapele Mahogany Accents	7,495	6,451
EU 122		48	Polished Ebony	6,895	6,015
EU 122		48	Polished Mahogany/Walnut/White	6,995	6,087
EU 122		48	Satin Cherry	6,995	6,087
EU 122S		48	Polished Ebony w/Silver Hardware	6,995	6,087
EU 122 Silent		48	Polished Ebony w/Silent System	9,295	7,760
EU 131		52	Polished Ebony	7,895	6,742

Grands

Model	Feet	Inches	Description	MSRP	SMP
GP 150	4	11	Hand-rubbed Satin Ebony	12,795	9,824
GP 150	4	11	Polished Ebony	12,195	9,410
GP 150	4	11	Polished Mahogany/Walnut/White	12,795	9,824
GP 150	4	11	Polished Sapele Mahogany/Artisan Walnut	13,495	10,307
GP 150SP	4	11	Polished Ebony w/Silver Plate/Hardware	12,795	9,824
GP 160	5	3	Hand-rubbed Satin Ebony	14,295	10,859
GP 160	5	3	Polished Ebony	13,795	10,514
GP 160SP	5	3	Polished Ebony w/Silver Plate/Hardware	14,295	10,859
GP 160	5	3	Polished Mahogany/Walnut/White	14,295	10,859
GP 160	5	3	Polished Sapele Mahogany/Artisan Walnut	14,995	11,341
GP 160 SP	5	3	Polished White w/Silver Plate/Hardware	15,295	11,548
GP 160SP	5	3	Polished Red w/Silver Plate/Hardware	16,295	12,238
GP 170	5	7	Hand-rubbed Satin Ebony	16,995	12,721
GP 170	5	7	Polished Ebony	16,295	12,238
GP 170	5	7	Polished Sapele Mahogany/Artisan Walnut	17,295	12,928
GP 188A	6	2	Polished Ebony	19,495	14,445

Model	Feet	Inches	Description	MSRP	SMP

PEARL RIVER (continued)

Model	Feet	Inches	Description	MSRP	SMP
GP 212	7		Polished Ebony	33,495	24,100
GP 275	9		Polished Ebony	96,995	67,893

PERZINA

Verticals

Model	Feet	Inches	Description	MSRP	SMP
GP-112 Kompact		45	Continental Polished Ebony	8,890	8,000
GP-112 Kompact		45	Continental Polished Walnut/Mahogany	9,450	8,250
GP-112 Kompact		45	Continental Polished White	9,780	8,490
GP-115 Merit		45	Polished Ebony	9,660	8,430
GP-115 Merit		45	Polished Mahogany/Walnut	10,220	8,690
GP-115 Merit		45	Polished White	10,550	8,900
GP-115 Merit		45	Queen Anne Polished Ebony	10,220	8,600
GP-115 Merit		45	Queen Anne Polished Mahogany/Walnut	11,045	8,920
GP-115 Merit		45	Queen Anne Polished White	11,375	9,140
GP-122 Konsumat		48	Polished Ebony	10,990	9,090
GP-122 Konsumat		48	Polished Ebony with Chrome Hardware	12,090	10,000
GP-122 Konsumat		48	Polished Mahogany/Walnut	11,375	9,400
GP-122 Konsumat		48	Polished White	11,580	9,590
GP-122 Konsumat		48	Queen Anne Polished Ebony	11,375	9,380
GP-122 Konsumat		48	Queen Anne Polished Mahogany/Walnut	12,200	9,590
GP-122 Konsumat		48	Queen Anne Polished White	12,500	9,800
GP-122 Balmoral		48	Designer Polished Ebony	12,285	9,300
GP-122 Balmoral		48	Designer Polished Ebony/Bubinga (two-tone)	13,300	10,840
GP-129 Kapitol		51	Polished Ebony	12,240	10,220
GP-129 Kapitol		51	Polished Mahogany/Walnut	12,860	10,420
GP-129 Kapitol		51	Polished White	13,520	10,630
GP-129 Kapitol		51	Queen Anne Polished Ebony	13,520	10,420
GP-129 Kapitol		51	Queen Anne Polished Mahogany/Walnut	13,565	10,630
GP-129 Kapitol		51	Queen Anne Polished White	14,290	10,840
GP-130 Konzert		52	Polished Ebony	14,840	11,460

Grands

Model	Feet	Inches	Description	MSRP	SMP
GBT-152 Prysm	5	1	Polished Ebony	17,260	16,440
GBT-152 Prysm	5	1	Polished Mahogany/Walnut	18,530	17,650
GBT-152 Prysm	5	1	Polished White	18,750	17,860
GBT-152 Prysm	5	1	Designer Polished Mahogany/Walnut with Burled Walnut Inlay	20,490	19,520
GBT-152 Prysm	5	1	Designer Queen Anne or Empire Polished Ebony	17,590	16,760
GBT-152 Prysm	5	1	Designer Queen Anne or Empire Polished Mahogany/Walnut	18,880	17,980
GBT-152 Prysm	5	1	Designer Queen Anne or Empire Polished White	19,090	18,180
GBT-160 Sylvr	5	4	Polished Ebony	19,630	18,690
GBT-160 Sylvr	5	4	Polished Mahogany/Walnut	20,840	19,850
GBT-160 Sylvr	5	4	Polished White	21,030	20,020

PIANOBUYER *Model & Price Supplement*

Model	Feet	Inches	Description	MSRP	SMP
PERZINA *(continued)*					
GBT-160 Sylvr	5	4	Designer Polished Mahogany/Walnut with Burled Walnut Inlay	26,180	24,930
GBT-160 Sylvr	5	4	Designer Queen Anne or Empire Polished Ebony	19,970	19,020
GBT-160 Sylvr	5	4	Designer Queen Anne or Empire Polished Mahogany/ Walnut	21,180	20,170
GBT-160 Sylvr	5	4	Designer Queen Anne or Empire Polished White	21,330	20,320
GBT-175 Granit	5	10	Polished Ebony	20,620	19,640
GBT-175 Granit	5	10	Polished Mahogany/Walnut	21,830	20,790
GBT-175 Granit	5	10	Polished White	22,030	20,980
GBT-175 Granit	5	10	Designer Polished Mahogany/Walnut with Burled Walnut Inlay	27,180	25,880
GBT-175 Granit	5	10	Designer Queen Anne or Empire Polished Walnut with Burled Walnut Inlay	20,960	19,960
GBT-175 Granit	5	10	Designer Queen Anne or Empire Polished Mahogany/ Walnut	22,180	21,120
GBT-175 Granit	5	10	Designer Queen Anne or Empire Polished White	22,370	21,300
GBT-187 Royal	6	2	Polished Ebony	21,620	20,590
GBT-187 Royal	6	2	Polished Mahogany/Walnut	22,840	21,750
GBT-187 Royal	6	2	Polished White	23,030	21,930
GBT-187 Royal	6	2	Designer Polished Mahogany/Walnut with Burled Walnut Inlay	28,160	26,820
GBT-187 Royal	6	2	Designer Queen Anne or Empire Polished Ebony	21,950	20,910
GBT-187 Royal	6	2	Designer Queen Anne or Empire Polished Mahogany/ Walnut	23,180	22,070
GBT-187 Royal	6	2	Designer Queen Anne or Empire Polished White	23,360	22,250

PETROF

Most models are also available in finishes other than those shown here.

Verticals

Model		Inches	Description	MSRP	SMP
P 118 C1		46.25	Chippendale Polished Ebony	29,247	20,824
P 118 D1		46.25	Demi-Chippendale Polished Ebony	28,494	20,294
P 118 G2		46.25	Polished Ebony	27,732	19,760
P 118 M1		46.25	Polished Ebony	26,397	18,820
P 118 P1		46.25	Polished Ebony	25,854	18,440
P 118 R1		46.25	Rococo Satin White w/Gold Trim	30,978	22,046
P 118 S1		46.25	Continental Polished Ebony/White	22,737	16,250
P 122 N1		47.75	Polished Ebony	27,014	19,240
P 125 F1		49.25	Polished Ebony	27,935	19,900
P 125 G1		49.25	Polished Ebony	29,487	20,990
P 125 M1		49.25	Polished Ebony	29,073	20,700
P 127 NEXT		49.5	Satin Ebony with Chrome Legs	40,924	29,030
P 127 NEXT		49.5	Satin Wood Tones with Chrome Legs	45,323	32,120
P 131 M1		51	Polished Ebony	39,920	28,326
P 135 K1		53	Polished Ebony	47,589	33,714

Model	Feet	Inches	Description	MSRP	SMP
PETROF *(continued)*					
Grands					
P 159	5	2	Bora Polished Ebony	78,567	55,480
P 159	5	2	Bora Demi-Chippendale Polished Ebony	84,860	58,778
P 173	5	6	Breeze Polished Ebony	82,790	58,448
P 173	5	6	Breeze Chippendale Polished Ebony	94,142	68,424
P 173	5	6	Breeze Demi-Chippendale Polished Ebony	91,805	68,780
P 173	5	6	Breeze Klasik Polished Ebony	92,363	70,776
P 173	5	6	Breeze Rococo Satin White w/Gold Trim	97,487	68,780
P 194	6	3	Storm Polished Ebony	86,903	61,336
P 194	6	3	Storm Styl Polished Ebony	99,422	70,136
P 210	6	10	Pasat Polished Ebony	124,190	87,500
P 237	7	9	Monsoon Polished Ebony	162,899	120,740
P 284	9	2	Mistral Polished Ebony	224,682	158,152
Grands			Mahogany/Walnut Upcharge	2,400	2,400
Grands			White or Color Upcharge	1,600	1,600
Petrof, Ant. Verticals					
136		53.5	Polished Ebony		34,600
Petrof, Ant. Grands					
225	7	4	Polished Ebony		167,320
275	9		Polished Ebony		225,400
PRAMBERGER					
Legacy Series Verticals					
LV-110		43	Continental Polished Ebony	7,719	5,498
LV-43F		43	French Provincial Satin Cherry	8,339	5,898
LV-43T		43	Satin Mahogany/Walnut	8,339	5,898
LV-115		45	Satin Ebony	9,059	6,298
LV-115		45	Polished Ebony	8,339	5,898
LV-115		45	Polished Mahogany/Walnut	9,269	6,398
LV-118		46.5	Satin Ebony	9,779	6,698
LV-118		46.5	Polished Ebony	9,059	6,298
Signature Series Verticals					
PV-118F/R/T		46.5	Decorator Satin Cherry/Mahogany/Walnut	10,299	6,998
PV-118S		46.5	Satin Ebony	10,609	7,198
PV-118S		46.5	Polished Ebony	9,989	6,798
PV-121		47.5	Satin Ebony	12,049	7,998
PV-121		47.5	Polished Ebony	11,329	7,598
PV-132		52	Satin Ebony	13,389	8,798
PV-132		52	Polished Ebony	12,669	8,398
J.P. Pramberger Platinum Series Verticals					
JP-132		52	Satin Ebony	16,789	10,798
JP-132		52	Polished Ebony	15,449	9,998

Model	Feet	Inches	Description	MSRP	SMP

PRAMBERGER *(continued)*
Legacy Series Grands

Model	Feet	Inches	Description	MSRP	SMP
LG-149	4	9	Satin Ebony	18,179	11,918
LG-149	4	9	Polished Ebony	16,809	11,098
LG-149	4	9	Polished Mahogany/Walnut	18,869	12,318
LG-157	5	2	Satin Ebony	20,599	12,798
LG-157	5	2	Polished Ebony	19,159	11,998
LG-157	5	2	Polished Ebony w/Bubinga or Pommele Accents	23,999	14,198
LG-157	5	2	Polished Fire Red	25,749	15,198
LG-175	5	9	Satin Ebony	25,339	14,598
LG-175	5	9	Polished Ebony	23,689	13,798

Signature Series Grands

Model	Feet	Inches	Description	MSRP	SMP
PS-157	5	2	Satin Ebony	25,439	15,198
PS-157	5	2	Polished Ebony	23,999	14,398
PS-157	5	2	Polished Ebony w/Bubinga or Pommele Accents	28,119	16,598
PS-175	5	9	Satin Ebony	27,499	16,398
PS-175	5	9	Polished Ebony	26,059	15,598
PS-185	6	1	Satin Ebony	28,529	16,998
PS-185	6	1	Polished Ebony	27,089	16,198
PS-208	6	10	Satin Ebony	38,049	21,798
PS-208	6	10	Polished Ebony	34,299	20,598

J.P. Pramberger Platinum Series Grands

Model	Feet	Inches	Description	MSRP	SMP
JP-179L	5	10	Satin Ebony	44,079	24,998
JP-179L	5	10	Polished Ebony	42,849	24,398
JP-179LF	5	10	French Provincial Satin Ebony	51,499	28,998
JP-179LF	5	10	French Provincial Lacquer Semigloss Cherry	51,499	28,998
JP-208B	6	10	Satin Ebony	55,929	31,398
JP-208B	6	10	Polished Ebony	54,799	30,798
JP-228C	7	6	Satin Ebony	60,869	34,198
JP-228C	7	6	Polished Ebony	60,249	33,798
JP-280E	9	2	Polished Ebony	179,839	98,998

RITMÜLLER
Performance Verticals

Model	Feet	Inches	Description	MSRP	SMP
UP 110RB		43	French Provincial Satin Cherry	7,195	5,797
UP 110RB1		43	Italian Provincial Satin Walnut	7,195	5,797
UP 110R2		43	Polished Ebony	5,495	4,663
UP 110R2		43	Polished Mahogany	5,595	4,730
UP 120RE		47	Satin Mahogany	8,395	6,597
UP 121RB		48	Polished Ebony	7,295	5,863
UP 121RB		48	Polished Mahogany/Walnut/White	7,795	6,197

Model	Feet	Inches	Description	MSRP	SMP

RITMÜLLER *(continued)*

Premium Verticals

Model	Feet	Inches	Description	MSRP	SMP
UH 121R		48	Chippendale Polished Ebony	10,295	7,863
UH 121R		48	Chippendale Polished Sapele Mahogany	10,695	8,130
UH 121RA		48	Polished Ebony	10,195	7,797
UH 121RA Silent		48	Polished Ebony w/Silent System	13,695	10,130
UH 132R		52	Polished Ebony	12,495	9,330

Performance Grands

Model	Feet	Inches	Description	MSRP	SMP
R8	4	11	Polished Ebony	14,495	10,663
R8 SP	4	11	Polished Ebony w/Silver Plate/Hardware	15,395	11,263
R8	4	11	Polished Mahogany/White	15,395	11,263
R9	5	3	Polished Ebony	15,995	11,663
R9	5	3	Polished Mahogany/White	16,495	11,997
R9 SP	5	3	Polished White w/Silver Plate/Hardware	17,495	12,663

Premium Grands

Model	Feet	Inches	Description	MSRP	SMP
GH 148R	4	10	Polished Ebony	17,195	12,463
GH 148R	4	10	Polished Sapele Mahogany	17,795	12,863
GH 160R	5	3	Hand-rubbed Satin Ebony	20,795	14,863
GH 160R	5	3	Polished Ebony	19,995	14,330
GH 160R	5	3	Polished Sapele Mahogany	20,795	14,863
GH 170R	5	7	Polished Ebony	21,995	15,663
GH 188R	6	2	Polished Ebony	26,995	18,997
GH 212R	7		Polished Ebony	33,495	23,330
GH 275R	9		Polished Ebony	96,995	65,663

RÖNISCH

Verticals

Model	Feet	Inches	Description	MSRP	SMP
118 K		47	Polished Ebony	22,428	22,428
118 K		47	Satin Mahogany/Walnut	23,604	23,604
118 K		47	Polished Mahogany/Walnut	27,720	27,720
118 K		47	Satin Cherry	24,024	24,024
118 K		47	Satin Beech/Alder/Ash/Oak	22,722	22,722
118 K		47	Polished White	24,570	24,570
118 K		47	Satin Swiss Pear/Indian Apple	24,654	24,654
118 KI		47	Polished Mahogany w/Vavona Inlays	28,770	28,770
118 KI		47	Polished Walnut w/Burled Walnut Inlays	28,980	28,980
118 KI		47	Polished Cherry w/Yew Inlays	29,400	29,400
125 K		49	Polished Ebony	24,780	24,780
125 K		49	Satin Mahogany/Walnut	25,830	25,830
125 K		49	Polished Mahogany/Walnut	30,198	30,198
125 K		49	Satin Cherry	25,746	25,746
125 K		49	Polished White	26,964	26,964
125 K		49	Satin Swiss Pear/Indian Apple	30,828	30,828
125 K		49	Carl Ronisch Edition Polished Burl Walnut	34,314	34,314

Model	Feet	Inches	Description	MSRP	SMP
RÖNISCH *(continued)*					
125 KI		49	Polished Mahogany w/Vavona Inlays	31,080	31,080
125 KI		49	Polished Walnut w/Burled Walnut Inlays	31,500	31,500
125 KI		49	Polished Cherry w/Yew Inlays	32,130	32,130
132 K		52	Polished Ebony	27,930	27,930
132 K		52	Satin Mahogany/Walnut	28,308	28,308
132 K		52	Polished Mahogany/Walnut	32,634	32,634
132 K		52	Polished White	30,114	30,114
132 K		52	Satin Swiss Pear/Indian Apple	33,936	33,936
132 K		52	Polished Bubinga	33,570	33,570
132 K		52	Carl Ronisch Edition Polished Burl Walnut	37,884	37,884
132 KI		52	Polished Mahogany w/Vavona Inlays	35,280	35,280
132 KI		52	Polished Walnut w/Burled Walnut Inlays	35,700	35,700
132 KI		52	Polished Cherry w/Yew Inlays	36,330	36,330
Grands					
175 K	5	9	Polished Ebony	68,894	68,894
175 K	5	9	Satin Mahogany/Walnut	70,452	70,452
175 K	5	9	Polished Mahogany/Walnut	81,438	81,438
175 K	5	9	Satin Cherry	73,568	73,568
175 K	5	9	Polished White	72,808	72,808
175 K	5	9	Polished Bubinga	85,728	85,728
175 K	5	9	Polished Rosewood	92,378	92,378
175 K	5	9	Carl Ronisch Edition Polished Burl Walnut	96,292	96,292
175 K	5	9	Carl Ronisch Edition Polished Vavona	96,292	96,292
175 K	5	9	Carl Ronisch Edition Polished Pyramid Mahogany	100,206	100,206
175 KI	5	9	Polished Mahogany w/Vavona Inlays	99,066	99,066
175 KI	5	9	Polished Walnut w/Burled Walnut Inlays	101,004	101,004
175 KI	5	9	Polished Cherry w/Yew Inlays	103,740	103,740
186 K	6	1	Polished Ebony	74,746	74,746
186 K	6	1	Satin Mahogany/Walnut	77,520	77,520
186 K	6	1	Polished Mahogany/Walnut	88,502	88,502
186 K	6	1	Satin Cherry	79,458	79,458
186 K	6	1	Polished White	78,660	78,660
186 K	6	1	Polished Bubinga	91,618	91,618
186 K	6	1	Polished Rosewood	98,268	98,268
186 K	6	1	Carl Ronisch Edition Polished Burl Walnut	102,182	102,182
186 K	6	1	Carl Ronisch Edition Polished Vavona	102,182	102,182
186 K	6	1	Carl Ronisch Edition Polished Pyramid Mahogany	106,096	106,096
186 KI	6	1	Polished Mahogany w/Vavona Inlays	104,956	104,956
186 KI	6	1	Polished Walnut w/Burled Walnut Inlays	107,274	107,274
186 KI	6	1	Polished Cherry w/Yew Inlays	110,390	110,390
210 K	6	10.5	Polished Ebony	86,156	86,156
210 K	6	10.5	Satin Mahogany/Walnut	89,080	89,080
210 K	6	10.5	Polished Mahogany/Walnut	98,600	98,600
210 K	6	10.5	Polished White	89,658	89,658
210 K	6	10.5	Polished Bubinga	108,800	108,800

Model	Feet	Inches	Description	MSRP	SMP

RÖNISCH (continued)

Model	Feet	Inches	Description	MSRP	SMP
210 K	6	10.5	Polished Rosewood	112,200	112,200
210 K	6	10.5	Carl Ronisch Edition Polished Burl Walnut	106,250	106,250
210 K	6	10.5	Carl Ronisch Edition Polished Vavona	106,250	106,250
210 K	6	10.5	Carl Ronisch Edition Polished Pyramid Mahogany	112,200	112,200
210 KI	6	10.5	Polished Mahogany w/Vavona Inlays	113,560	113,560
210 KI	6	10.5	Polished Walnut w/Burled Walnut Inlays	116,960	116,960
210 KI	6	10.5	Polished Cherry w/Yew Inlays	120,360	120,360

SAMICK

Verticals

Model	Inches	Description	MSRP	SMP
JS-43	43	Continental Satin Ebony	8,549	6,158
JS-43	43	Continental Polished Ebony	7,719	5,638
JS-143F	43	French Provincial Satin Cherry	8,549	6,158
JS-143T	43	Satin Mahogany	8,549	6,158
JS-115	45	Satin Ebony	9,269	6,358
JS-115	45	Polished Ebony	8,549	6,158
JS-115	45	Polished Mahogany/Walnut	9,059	6,458
JS-247	46.5	Institutional Satin Ebony	11,019	7,598
JS-247	46.5	Institutional Polished Ebony	10,299	7,178
JS-247	46.5	Institutional Satin Walnut	11,019	7,598
JS-118H	46.5	Satin Ebony	9,989	6,978
JS-118H	46.5	Polished Ebony	9,269	6,558
JS-121M	48	Satin Ebony	11,019	7,598
JS-121M	48	Polished Ebony	10,299	7,178
JS-132	52	Satin Ebony	13,389	8,939
JS-132	52	Polished Ebony	12,359	8,418

Grands

Model	Feet	Inches	Description	MSRP	SMP
SIG-49	4	9	Satin Ebony	18,179	11,918
SIG-49	4	9	Polished Ebony	16,809	11,098
SIG-54	5	4	Satin Ebony	21,629	13,978
SIG-54	5	4	Polished Ebony	19,569	12,638
SIG-54	5	4	Polished Fire-Engine Red	26,469	16,858
SIG-54	5	4	Polished Ebony w/Bubinga or Pommele Accents	24,509	15,738
SIG-57	5	7	Satin Ebony	25,029	16,038
SIG-57	5	7	Polished Ebony	23,479	15,118
SIG-57L	5	7	Empire Satin Ebony	27,809	17,698
SIG-57L	5	7	Empire Polished Ebony	26,469	16,858
SIG-61	6	1	Satin Ebony	27,089	17,278
SIG-61	6	1	Polished Ebony	25,439	16,258
SIG-61L	6	1	Empire Satin Ebony	29,659	18,818
SIG-61L	6	1	Empire Polished Ebony	28,119	17,898

Model	Feet	Inches	Description	MSRP	SMP

SAMICK *(continued)*
NSG Series Grands

Model	Feet	Inches	Description	MSRP	SMP
NSG 158	5	2	Satin Ebony	25,495	19,198
NSG 158	5	2	Polished Ebony	23,995	18,198
NSG 175	5	7	Satin Ebony	27,995	20,998
NSG 175	5	7	Polished Ebony	26,495	19,998
NSG 186	6	1	Satin Ebony	30,795	22,998
NSG 186	6	1	Polished Ebony	29,395	21,998

SAUTER
Standard wood veneers are walnut, mahogany, ash, and alder.
Verticals

Model	Feet	Inches	Description	MSRP	SMP
119		46	Peter Maly Concent Satin Ebony	32,000	32,000
119		46	Peter Maly Concent Polished Ebony	34,000	34,000
122		48	Ragazza Polished Ebony	36,500	36,500
122		48	Ragazza Satin Cherry	36,500	36,500
122		48	Ragazza Polished Cherry/Yew	43,000	43,000
122		48	Vista Polished Ebony	40,000	40,000
122		48	Vista Satin Maple	38,500	38,500
122		48	Vista Satin Cherry	40,000	40,000
122		48	Master Class Polished Ebony	47,000	47,000
122		48	Peter Maly Artes Polished Ebony	52,000	52,000
122		48	Peter Maly Artes Polished Palisander/Macassar	53,500	53,500
122		48	Peter Maly Artes Polished White	53,500	53,500
122		48	Peter Maly Pure Noble Polished Ebony/Veneers	49,000	49,000
122		48	Peter Maly Pure Noble Polished White/Red	50,000	50,000
122		48	Peter Maly Pure Basic Satin Ebony/Walnut	39,900	39,900
122		48	Peter Maly Pure Basic Satin White	39,900	39,900
122		48	Peter Maly Pure Basic Satin White/Maple	39,900	39,900
122		48	Peter Maly Rondo Polished Ebony	43,500	43,500
122		48	Peter Maly Rondo Satin Wenge	40,500	40,500
122		48	Peter Maly Vitrea Colored Ebony with Glass	41,000	41,000
122		48	Schulpiano Satin Beech/Black Ash	32,000	32,000
130		51	Master Class Polished Ebony	53,000	53,000
130		51	Competence Polished Ebony	45,500	45,500
130		51	Competence Satin Walnut	43,000	43,000
130		51	Sonder Polished Ebony w/Sostenuto	39,900	39,900
130		51	Sonder Polished Ebony w/o Sostenuto	36,000	36,000

Grands

Model	Feet	Inches	Description	MSRP	SMP
160	5	3	Alpha Polished Ebony	95,000	95,000
160	5	3	Alpha Satin Standard Wood Veneers	88,000	88,000
160	5	3	Chippendale Satin Cherry	99,000	99,000
160	5	3	Chippendale Satin Standard Wood Veneers	96,000	96,000
160	5	3	Noblesse Satin Cherry	106,000	106,000

Model	Feet	Inches	Description	MSRP	SMP

SAUTER (continued)

Model	Feet	Inches	Description	MSRP	SMP
160	5	3	Noblesse Polished Cherry	115,000	115,000
160	5	3	Noblesse Satin Burl Walnut	111,000	111,000
160	5	3	Noblesse Satin Standard Wood Veneers	106,000	106,000
160	5	3	Noblesse Polished Standard Wood Veneers	114,000	114,000
185	6	1	Delta Polished Ebony	106,000	106,000
185	6	1	Delta Polished Ebony w/Burl Walnut	110,000	110,000
185	6	1	Delta Polished Pyramid Mahogany	117,000	117,000
185	6	1	Delta Polished Bubinga	116,000	116,000
185	6	1	Delta Polished Rio Palisander	117,000	117,000
185	6	1	Delta Satin Maple with Silver	99,000	99,000
185	6	1	Delta Polished White	110,000	110,000
185	6	1	Delta Satin Standard Wood Veneers	98,000	98,000
185	6	1	Chippendale Satin Cherry	109,000	109,000
185	6	1	Chippendale Satin Standard Wood Veneers	105,000	105,000
185	6	1	Noblesse Satin Cherry	116,000	116,000
185	6	1	Noblesse Polished Cherry	129,000	129,000
185	6	1	Noblesse Satin Burl Walnut	121,000	121,000
185	6	1	Noblesse Satin Standard Wood Veneers	112,000	112,000
185	6	1	Noblesse Polished Standard Wood Veneers	126,000	126,000
210	6	11	Peter Maly Vivace Polished Ebony	150,000	150,000
210	6	11	Peter Maly Vivace Satin Wood Veneers	140,000	140,000
210	6	11	Peter Maly Vivace Polished White	150,000	150,000
220	7	3	Omega Polished Ebony	135,000	135,000
220	7	3	Omega Polished Burl Walnut	149,000	149,000
220	7	3	Omega Polished Pyramid Mahogany	148,000	148,000
220	7	3	Omega Satin Standard Wood Veneers	129,000	129,000
230	7	7	Peter Maly Ambiente Polished Ebony	170,000	170,000
230	7	7	Peter Maly Ambiente Polished Ebony w/Crystals	195,000	195,000
275	9		Concert Polished Ebony	230,000	230,000

SCHIMMEL

Classic Series Verticals

Model		Inches	Description	MSRP	SMP
C 116		46	Tradition Polished Ebony	24,915	20,932
C 116		46	Tradition Polished Mahogany/White	28,083	23,466
C 116		46	Tradition Satin Walnut/Cherry/Beech/Alder	24,915	20,932
C 116		46	Modern Polished Ebony	28,875	24,100
C 116		46	Modern Polished White	32,043	26,634
C 116		46	Modern Cubus Polished Ebony	28,875	24,100
C 116		46	Modern Cubus Polished White	32,043	26,634
C 120		48	Tradition Polished Ebony	27,028	22,622
C 120		48	Tradition Polished Mahogany/White	30,195	25,156
C 120		48	Tradition Satin Walnut/Cherry/Beech/Alder	27,028	22,622
C 120		48	Tradition Marketerie Polished Mahogany w/Inlay	32,305	26,844
C 120		48	Elegance Manhattan Polished Ebony	26,105	21,884

Model	Feet	Inches	Description	MSRP	SMP
SCHIMMEL *(continued)*					
C 120		48	Elegance Manhattan Polished Mahogany/White	29,273	24,418
C 120		48	Royal Polished Ebony	29,665	24,732
C 120		48	Royal Intarsie Flora Polished Mahogany w/Inlays	34,945	28,956
C 121		48	Tradition Polished Ebony	27,705	23,164
C 121		48	Tradition Polished Mahogany	30,950	25,760
C 121		48	Elegance Manhattan Polished Ebony	26,758	22,406
C 121		48	Elegance Manhattan Polished Mahogany	30,005	25,004
C 123		48	Tradition Polished Ebony (limited edition)	29,863	24,890
C 126		50	Tradition Polished Ebony	32,833	27,266
C 126		50	Tradition Polished Mahogany/White	36,000	29,800
C 130		51	Tradition Polished Ebony	35,473	29,378
C 130		51	Tradition Polished Mahogany/White	38,640	31,912

Konzert Series Verticals

Model	Feet	Inches	Description	MSRP	SMP
K 122		48	Elegance Polished Ebony	36,398	30,118
K 125		49	Tradition Polished Ebony	39,038	32,230
K 125		49	Tradition Polished Mahogany	43,260	35,608
K 132		52	Tradition Polished Ebony	44,580	36,664
K 132		52	Tradition Polished Mahogany	48,803	40,042

Fridolin Schimmel Verticals

Model	Feet	Inches	Description	MSRP	SMP
F 116		46	Polished Ebony	7,838	7,270
F 116		46	Polished White	8,213	7,570
F 121		48	Polished Ebony	8,963	8,170
F 121		48	Polished Walnut/White	9,338	8,470
F 123		49	Polished Ebony	10,088	9,070
F 123		49	Polished Mahogany/White	10,463	9,370

Wilhelm Schimmel Verticals

Model	Feet	Inches	Description	MSRP	SMP
W 114		46	Tradition Polished Ebony	17,130	14,704
W 114		46	Tradition Polished Mahogany/White	19,770	16,816
W 114		46	Modern Polished Ebony	18,050	15,440
W 114		46	Modern Polished White	20,075	17,060
W 118		48	Tradition Polished Ebony	18,715	15,972
W 118		48	Tradition Polished Mahogany/White	21,353	18,082
W 123		49	Tradition Polished Ebony	20,298	17,238
W 123		49	Tradition Polished Mahogany/White	22,938	19,350
W 123		49	Tradition Polished Ebony	20,298	17,238
W 123		49	Tradition Polished Mahogany/White	22,938	19,350

Classic Series Grands

Model	Feet	Inches	Description	MSRP	SMP
C 169	5	7	Tradition Polished Ebony	67,938	55,350
C 169	5	7	Tradition Polished Mahogany/White	74,535	60,628
C 189	6	2	Tradition Polished Ebony	71,895	58,516
C 189	6	2	Tradition Polished Mahogany/White	78,495	63,796
C 213	7		Tradition Polished Ebony	78,495	63,796
C 213	7		Tradition Polished Mahogany/White	85,093	69,074

Model	Feet	Inches	Description	MSRP	SMP

SCHIMMEL *(continued)*
Konzert Series Grands

Model	Feet	Inches	Description	MSRP	SMP
K 175	5	9	Tradition Polished Ebony	86,870	70,496
K 175	5	9	Tradition Polished Mahogany/White	94,558	76,646
K 195	6	4	Tradition Polished Ebony	94,558	76,646
K 195	6	4	Tradition Polished Mahogany/White	102,245	82,796
K 213	7		Glas Clear Acrylic and White or Black and Gold	320,313	257,250
K 213	7		Otmar Alt Polished Ebony w/Color Motifs	230,625	185,500
K 219	7	2	Tradition Polished Ebony	102,245	82,796
K 219	7	2	Tradition Polished Mahogany/White	109,933	88,946
K 230	7	6	Tradition Polished Ebony	117,620	95,096
K 256	8	4	Tradition Polished Ebony	132,995	107,396
K 280	9	2	Tradition Polished Ebony	153,495	123,796

Wilhelm Schimmel Grands

Model	Feet	Inches	Description	MSRP	SMP
W 180	6		Tradition Polished Ebony	41,413	34,130
W 180	6		Tradition Polished Mahogany/White	46,693	38,354
W 206	6	10	Tradition Polished Ebony	50,650	41,520
W 206	6	10	Tradition Polished Mahogany/White	55,930	45,744

SCHULZ, GEBR.
Verticals

Model	Feet	Inches	Description	MSRP	SMP
G-20		48	Polished Ebony	9,995	9,590
G-20		48	Hand-rubbed Satin Walnut	12,895	12,500

Grands

Model	Feet	Inches	Description	MSRP	SMP
G-58	5	5	Polished Ebony	18,995	18,995
G-86	6		Polished Ebony	23,995	23,995
G-288	9		Polished Ebony	49,995	49,995

SCHULZE POLLMANN
Studio Series Verticals

Model	Feet	Inches	Description	MSRP	SMP
SU118A		46	Polished Peacock Ebony	15,995	9,490
SU118A		46	Polished Peacock Mahogany/Walnut	16,995	10,090
SU122A		48	Polished Peacock Ebony	18,995	10,890
SU122A		48	Polished Peacock Mahogany/Walnut	19,995	11,490
SU122A		48	Polished Feather Mahogany	20,995	12,090
SU132A		52	Polished Peacock Ebony	23,995	13,490

Academy Series Verticals

Model	Feet	Inches	Description	MSRP	SMP
A-125E		50	Polished Ebony	26,995	14,890
A-125E		50	Polished Peacock Ebony	27,995	15,490
A-125E		50	Polished Peacock Mahogany	30,995	17,490
A-125E		50	Polished Peacock Walnut	31,995	18,090
A-125E		50	Polished Feather Mahogany	33,995	18,090

Model	Feet	Inches	Description	MSRP	SMP

SCHULZE POLLMANN *(continued)*
Studio Series Grands

Model	Feet	Inches	Description	MSRP	SMP
S148	4	10	Polished Ebony	18,995	18,490
SU148	4	10	Polished Peacock Ebony/Feather Mahogany	19,995	19,490
S160	5	3	Polished Ebony	21,995	20,090
SU160	5	3	Polished Peacock Ebony/Feather Mahogany	22,995	21,090
S172A	5	8	Polished Ebony	24,995	22,490
SU172A	5	8	Polished Peacock Ebony/Feather Mahogany	25,995	23,490
S187A	6	2	Polished Ebony	27,995	25,490
SU187A	6	2	Polished Peacock Ebony/Feather Mahogany	28,995	27,490

Masterpiece Series Grands

Model	Feet	Inches	Description	MSRP	SMP
160/GK	5	3	Polished Ebony (spade leg)	55,995	55,995
160/GK	5	3	Polished Briar Mahogany (spade leg)	59,995	59,995
160/GK	5	3	Polished Feather Mahogany (spade leg)	63,995	63,995
197/G5	6	6	Polished Ebony (spade leg)	77,995	76,990
197/G5	6	6	Polished Briar Mahogany (spade leg)	80,995	80,995
197/G5	6	6	Polished Feather Mahogany (spade leg)	84,995	84,995

SCHUMANN
Verticals

Model	Feet	Inches	Description	MSRP	SMP
C1-112		44	Polished Ebony	5,995	4,990
C1-112		44	Polished Mahogany	6,195	5,390
K1-122		48	Polished Ebony	6,495	5,590
K1-122		48	Polished Mahogany	6,695	5,990
K1-122		48	Polished Walnut/White	6,695	6,190

Grands

Model	Feet	Inches	Description	MSRP	SMP
GP-152	5		Polished Ebony	11,900	9,590
GP-152	5		Polished Mahogany/White	12,900	10,390
GP-168	5	6	Polished Ebony	14,900	11,990
GP-168	5	6	Polished White	15,900	12,590
GP-186	6	2	Polished Ebony	18,995	13,190

SEILER
Seiler Verticals

Model	Feet	Inches	Description	MSRP	SMP
SE-112		43	Modern, Satin Ebony	36,189	27,778
SE-116		45	Primus, Polished Ebony	29,769	23,038
SE-116		45	Mondial, Polished Ebony	31,409	24,278
SE-116		45	Mondial, Polished Rosewood	42,539	32,518
SE-116		45	Konsole, Polished Ebony	34,595	26,598
SE-116		45	Konzept6, Satin White	41,759	31,898
SE-116		45	Impuls, Polished Ebony	37,579	28,818
SE-116		45	Impuls, Satin Wenge	38,979	29,838
SE-116		45	Clou, Polished Ebony	36,979	28,398

Model	Feet	Inches	Description	MSRP	SMP

SEILER *(continued)*

Model	Feet	Inches	Description	MSRP	SMP
SE-116		45	Accent, Polished Ebony	36,979	28,398
SE-122		48	Primus, Polished Ebony	39,759	30,458
SE-126		49	Konsole, Polished Ebony	43,979	33,558
SE-126		49	Konsole, Satin Walnut	45,319	34,578
SE-126		49	Attraction, Polished Ebony	47,069	35,818
SE-126		49	Attraction, Polished Ebony w/Ziricote	61,249	46,318
SE-132		52	Consert, Polished Ebony	53,969	40,978
SE-132		52	Consert, Polished Ebony w/SMR	56,749	43,038
SE-132		52	Consert, Polished Ebony w/Rec Panel	56,749	43,038
SE-132		52	Consert, Polished Ebony w/Rec Panel/SMR	59,529	45,098

Eduard Seiler ED Series Verticals

Model	Feet	Inches	Description	MSRP	SMP
ED-126		49	Primus, Satin Ebony	13,499	10,998
ED-126		49	Primus, Polished Ebony	12,960	10,598
ED-126M		49	Primus, Satin Ebony w/SMR	14,850	11,998
ED-126M		49	Primus, Polished Ebony w/SMR	14,299	11,598
ED-132		52	Konzert, Satin Ebony	14,299	11,598
ED-132		52	Konzert, Polished Ebony	13,790	11,198
ED-132M		52	Konzert, Satin Ebony w/SMR	15,930	12,798
ED-132M		52	Konzert, Polished Ebony w/SMR	15,199	12,198

Eduard Seiler ES Studio Series Verticals

Model	Feet	Inches	Description	MSRP	SMP
ES-126		49	Primus, Satin Ebony	28,995	22,990
ES-126		49	Primus, Polished Ebony	27,495	21,990
ES-132		52	Konzert, Satin Ebony	32,095	24,990
ES-132		52	Konzert, Polished Ebony	30,595	24,190

Johannes Seiler Verticals

Model	Feet	Inches	Description	MSRP	SMP
GS-110NDR		43	Continental Polished Ebony	9,639	9,198
GS-110NDR		43	Continental Polished Lacquer Dark Walnut	10,099	9,598
GS-110NDR		43	Continental Polished Fire-Engine Red	10,099	9,598
GS-110BDR		43	170th Anniv. Polished Grey w/Black Hardware	10,099	9,598
GS-110BDR		43	170th Anniv. Polished White w/Black Hardware	10,099	9,598
GS-112NDR		44	Polished Ebony	10,099	9,598
GS-112NDR		44	Polished Lacquer Dark Walnut	10,590	9,998
GS-112NDR		44	Polished Fire-Engine Red	10,590	9,998
GS-112BDR		44	170th Anniv. Polished White/Grey w/Black Hardware	10,590	9,998
GS-116N		45.5	Satin Ebony w/Nickel Hardware	9,779	8,640
GS-116N		45.5	Polished Ebony w/Nickel Hardware	9,679	8,240
GS-247		46.5	Satin Ebony	10,509	9,240
GS-247		46.5	Polished Ebony	9,779	8,640
GS-247		46.5	Satin Walnut	10,509	9,240
GS-118		47	Satin Ebony	9,989	8,840
GS-118		47	Polished Ebony	9,289	8,440
GS-121		47.5	Ditto, Polished Ebony w/Silver accent	11,949	9,840
GS-122		48.5	Satin Ebony	10,995	9,440
GS-122		48.5	Polished Ebony	9,989	8,840

PIANOBUYER *Model & Price Supplement*

Model	Feet	Inches	Description	MSRP	SMP
SEILER *(continued)*					
GS-122N		48.5	Impulz, Polished Ebony	10,290	9,198
GS-122LID		48.5	Satin Dark Walnut	11,250	9,64
Seiler Grands					
SE-168	5	6	Virtuoso, Polished Ebony	99,289	74,538
SE-168	5	6	Virtuoso, Polished Mahogany	119,269	89,378
SE-186	6	2	Maestro, Polished Ebony	116,599	87,318
SE-186	6	2	Maestro, Polished Mahogany	124,939	93,498
SE-186	6	2	Maestro, Polished Rosewood	133,489	99,878
SE-186	6	2	Maestro, Matte Ebony Ceramic	139,189	103,998
SE-186	6	2	Maestro, Polished Ebony w/Ziricote	126,279	94,538
SE-186	6	2	Louvre, Polished Cherry	157,489	117,598
SE-186	6	2	Florenz, Polished Mahogany	157,489	117,598
SE-208	6	10	Professional, Polished Ebony	130,709	97,818
SE-242	8		Konzert, Polished Ebony	172,939	129,138
SE-278	9	2	Konzert, Polished Ebony	280,879	209,058
Eduard Seiler ED Series Grands					
ED-168	5	6	Virtuoso, Satin Ebony	37,720	28,940
ED-168	5	6	Virtuoso, Polished Ebony	37,180	28,540
ED-168HS	5	6	Heritage, Satin Ebony	46,999	35,798
ED-168HS	5	6	Heritage, Polished Ebony	45,759	34,998
ED-186	6	2	Maestro, Satin Ebony	45,890	34,800
ED-186	6	2	Maestro, Polished Ebony	44,550	34,000
ED-208	6	10	Conservatory Artist, Satin Ebony	63,179	47,798
ED-208	6	10	Conservatory Artist, Polished Ebony	58,320	44,198
Eduard Seiler ES Studio Series Grands					
ES-168	5	6	Virtuoso, Satin Ebony	61,079	46,598
ES-168	5	6	Virtuoso, Polished Ebony	59,579	45,198
ES-186	6	2	Maestro, Satin Ebony	66,599	52,598
ES-186	6	2	Maestro, Polished Ebony	65,099	51,198
Johannes Seiler Grands					
GS-150	5		Satin Ebony	18,549	14,418
GS-150	5		Polished Ebony	17,919	13,358
GS-150	5		Polished White/Fire-Engine Red	20,389	15,418
GS-150	5		Polished Ebony w/Bubinga Accents	20,389	15,418
GS-150	5		Polished Lacquer Dark Walnut	19,649	14,998
GS-150B	5		170th Anniv. Polished Grey w/Black Hardware	20,389	15,418
GS-150LN	5		Satin Ebony w/Nickel Hardware, round leg	21,629	16,458
GS-150LN	5		Polished Ebony w/Nickel Hardware, round leg	20,389	15,418
GS-150LN	5		Polished Ebony w/Bubinga Accents & Nickel Hardware, round leg	22,119	16,858
GS-160	5	3	Satin Ebony	25,395	19,798
GS-160	5	3	Polished Ebony	23,995	18,798
GS-160LN	5	3	Satin Ebony, round leg	28,595	22,198

Model	Feet	Inches	Description	MSRP	SMP
SEILER *(continued)*					
GS-160LN	5	3	Polished Ebony, round leg	27,295	21,198
GS-175	5	9	Satin Ebony	27,795	21,598
GS-175	5	9	Polished Ebony	26,395	20,598
GS-186	6	2	Satin Ebony	29,695	22,998
GS-186	6	2	Polished Ebony	28,595	22,198
GS-208	6	10	Satin Ebony	32,649	26,038
GS-208	6	10	Polished Ebony	31,499	24,998

STEINBERG, G.

Verticals

Model	Feet	Inches	Description	MSRP	SMP
RH-111 Nicosia		45	Polished Ebony	7,580	7,220
RH-111 Nicosia		45	Polished Mahogany/Walnut	7,800	7,430
RH-111 Nicosia		45	Polished White	8,020	7,640
RH-115 Slate		45	Polished Ebony	7,800	7,430
RH-115 Slate		45	Polished Mahogany/Walnut	7,930	7,550
RH-115 Slate		45	Polished White	8,170	7,780
RH-115 Slate		45	Queen Anne Polished Ebony	7,930	7,550
RH-115 Slate		45	Queen Anne Polished Mahogany/Walnut	8,040	7,660
RH-115 Slate		45	Queen Anne Polished White	8,280	7,880
RH-119 Splendit		47	Polished Ebony	8,250	7,860
RH-119 Splendit		47	Polished Mahogany/Walnut	8,480	8,070
RH-119 Splendit		47	Polished White	8,690	8,280
RH-119 Splendit		47	Queen Anne Polished Ebony	8,370	7,970
RH-119 Splendit		47	Queen Anne Polished Mahogany/Walnut	8,590	8,180
RH-119 Splendit		47	Queen Anne Polished White	8,790	8,380
RH-123 Performance		49	Polished Ebony	8,480	8,070
RH-123 Performance		49	Queen Anne Polished Ebony	8,690	8,280
RH-126 Sienna		50	Polished Ebony	9,130	8,700
RH-126 Sienna		50	Queen Anne Polished Ebony	9,340	8,900

Grands

Model	Feet	Inches	Description	MSRP	SMP
GBT-152 Sovereign	5	1	Polished Ebony	15,450	14,710
GBT-152 Sovereign	5	1	Polished Mahogany/Walnut	16,610	15,820
GBT-152 Sovereign	5	1	Polished White	16,970	16,160
GBT-152 Sovereign	5	1	Queen Anne or Empire Polished Ebony	15,880	15,120
GBT-152 Sovereign	5	1	Queen Anne or Empire Polished Mahogany/Walnut	17,110	16,290
GBT-152 Sovereign	5	1	Queen Anne or Empire Polished White	17,390	16,560
GBT-160 Stockholm	5	5	Polished Ebony	17,750	16,910
GBT-160 Stockholm	5	5	Polished Mahogany/Walnut	18,850	17,950
GBT-160 Stockholm	5	5	Polished White	19,070	18,160
GBT-160 Stockholm	5	5	Queen Anne or Empire Polished Ebony	18,050	17,190
GBT-160 Stockholm	5	5	Queen Anne or Empire Polished Mahogany/Walnut	19,370	18,450
GBT-160 Stockholm	5	5	Queen Anne or Empire Polished White	19,590	18,660
GBT-175 Schwerin	5	10	Polished Ebony	18,490	17,620

Model	Feet	Inches	Description	MSRP	SMP

STEINBERG, G. *(continued)*

Model	Feet	Inches	Description	MSRP	SMP
GBT-175 Schwerin	5	10	Polished Mahogany/Walnut	20,040	19,080
GBT-175 Schwerin	5	10	Polished White	20,250	19,280
GBT-175 Schwerin	5	10	Queen Anne or Empire Polished Ebony	19,070	18,160
GBT-175 Schwerin	5	10	Queen Anne or Empire Polished Mahogany/Walnut	20,380	19,410
GBT-175 Schwerin	5	10	Queen Anne or Empire Polished White	20,590	19,620
GBT-187 Amsterdam	6	2	Polished Ebony	19,730	18,790
GBT-187 Amsterdam	6	2	Polished Mahogany/Walnut	20,820	19,820
GBT-187 Amsterdam	6	2	Polished White	21,030	20,030
GBT-187 Amsterdam	6	2	Queen Anne or Empire Polished Ebony	20,060	19,100
GBT-187 Amsterdam	6	2	Queen Anne or Empire Polished Mahogany/Walnut	21,260	20,240
GBT-187 Amsterdam	6	2	Queen Anne or Empire Polished White	21,470	20,450

STEINBERG, WILH.

Performance Series Verticals

Model	Feet	Inches	Description	MSRP	SMP
P118		46	Polished Ebony	8,280	6,590
P118		46	Polished White	9,390	7,290
P118C		46	Polished Ebony w/Chrome Hardware	8,490	6,690
P118C		46	Polished White w/Chrome Hardware	9,490	7,390
P121		48	Polished Ebony	9,490	7,390
P121		48	Polished White	10,490	8,090
P125E		50	Polished Ebony	10,990	8,590
P125EC		50	Polished Ebony w/Chrome Hardware	11,490	8,690

Signature Series Verticals

Model	Feet	Inches	Description	MSRP	SMP
S117		46	Polished Ebony	28,490	20,190
S117		46	Polished White	30,990	21,790
S117		46	Satin Mahogany/Walnut	31,490	21,990
S117		46	Polished Alder/Ash	32,190	22,490
S125		49	Polished Ebony	31,990	22,990
S125		49	Polished White	34,990	24,790
S125		49	Satin Mahogany/Walnut	35,990	24,990
S125		49	Polished Alder/Ash	34,990	25,690
S130		51	Polished Ebony	37,990	26,990
S130		51	Polished White	40,990	28,990
S130		51	Satin Mahogany/Walnut	42,190	29,190
S130		51	Polished Alder/Ash	43,590	30,090

Performance Series Grands

Model	Feet	Inches	Description	MSRP	SMP
P152	5		Polished Ebony	19,990	14,590
P152	5		Polished White	21,990	15,890
P165	5	5	Polished Ebony	23,490	16,990

Model	Feet	Inches	Description	MSRP	SMP

STEINBERG, WILH. *(continued)*

Model	Feet	Inches	Description	MSRP	SMP
P165	5	5	Polished White	25,490	18,290
P178	5	10	Polished Ebony	32,490	22,990

Signature Series Grands

Model	Feet	Inches	Description	MSRP	SMP
S188	6	2	Polished Ebony	79,990	54,980
S212	6	11	Polished Ebony	88,990	60,980

STEINGRAEBER & SÖHNE

Prices include bench.

Verticals

Model	Inches	Description	MSRP	SMP
122 T	48	Satin and Polished Ebony	49,460	48,210
122 T	48	Satin and Polished White	50,410	49,160
122 T	48	Polished Ebony w/Twist & Change Panels	55,720	54,470
122 T	48	Satin Ordinary Veneers	60,220	58,970
122 T	48	Polished Ordinary Veneers	66,160	64,910
122 T	48	Satin Special Veneers	62,270	61,020
122 T	48	Polished Special Veneers	68,200	66,950
122 T	48	Satin Extraordinary Veneers	75,500	74,250
122 T	48	Polished Extraordinary Veneers	81,450	80,200
122 T-SFM	48	Satin and Polished Ebony	52,260	51,010
122 T-SFM	48	Satin and Polished White	53,200	51,950
122 T-SFM	48	Polished Ebony w/Twist & Change Panels	58,510	57,260
122 T-SFM	48	Satin Ordinary Veneers	63,030	61,780
122 T-SFM	48	Polished Ordinary Veneers	68,930	67,680
122 T-SFM	48	Satin Special Veneers	65,070	63,820
122 T-SFM	48	Polished Special Veneers	70,970	69,720
122 T-SFM	48	Satin Extraordinary Veneers	78,300	77,050
122 T-SFM	48	Polished Extraordinary Veneers	84,260	83,010
130 T-PS	51	Satin and Polished Ebony	62,900	61,650
130 T-PS	51	Satin and Polished White	63,850	62,600
130 T-PS	51	Polished Ebony w/Twist & Change Panels	69,140	67,890
130 T-PS	51	Satin Ordinary Veneers	73,680	72,430
130 T-PS	51	Polished Ordinary Veneers	79,580	78,330
130 T-PS	51	Satin Special Veneers	75,670	74,420
130 T-PS	51	Polished Special Veneers	81,660	80,410
130 T-PS	51	Satin Extraordinary Veneers	88,960	87,710
130 T-PS	51	Polished Extraordinary Veneers	94,890	93,640
130 T-SFM	51	Satin and Polished Ebony	64,140	62,890
130 T-SFM	51	Satin and Polished White	65,070	63,820
130 T-SFM	51	Polished Ebony w/Twist & Change Panels	70,360	69,110
130 T-SFM	51	Satin Ordinary Veneers	74,890	73,640
130 T-SFM	51	Polished Ordinary Veneers	80,800	79,550
130 T-SFM	51	Satin Special Veneers	76,910	75,660
130 T-SFM	51	Polished Special Veneers	82,830	81,580
130 T-SFM	51	Satin Extraordinary Veneers	90,200	88,950

Model	Feet	Inches	Description	MSRP	SMP

STEINGRAEBER & SÖHNE *(continued)*

Model	Feet	Inches	Description	MSRP	SMP
130 T-SFM		51	Polished Extraordinary Veneers	96,100	94,850
138 K		54	Satin and Polished Ebony	66,680	65,430
138 K		54	Satin and Polished White	67,630	66,380
138 K		54	Polished Ebony w/Twist & Change Panels	72,920	71,670
138 K		54	Satin Ordinary Veneers	77,460	76,210
138 K		54	Polished Ordinary Veneers	83,360	82,110
138 K		54	Satin Special Veneers	79,470	78,220
138 K		54	Polished Special Veneers	85,390	84,140
138 K		54	Satin Extraordinary Veneers	92,720	91,470
138 K		54	Polished Extraordinary Veneers	98,670	97,420
138 K-SFM		54	Satin and Polished Ebony	69,480	68,230
138 K-SFM		54	Satin and Polished White	70,420	69,170
138 K-SFM		54	Polished Ebony w/Twist & Change Panels	75,730	74,480
138 K-SFM		54	Satin Ordinary Veneers	80,250	79,000
138 K-SFM		54	Polished Ordinary Veneers	86,150	84,900
138 K-SFM		54	Satin Special Veneers	82,290	81,040
138 K-SFM		54	Polished Special Veneers	88,210	86,960
138 K-SFM		54	Satin Extraordinary Veneers	95,540	94,290
138 K-SFM		54	Polished Extraordinary Veneers	101,460	100,210

Grands

Model	Feet	Inches	Description	MSRP	SMP
A-170	5	7	Satin and Polished Ebony	115,730	114,480
A-170	5	7	Satin and Polished White	118,270	117,020
A-170	5	7	Satin and Polished Ordinary Veneers	131,500	130,250
A-170	5	7	Satin and Polished Special Veneers	133,250	132,000
A-170	5	7	Satin and Polished Extraordinary Veneers	142,460	141,210
A-170 S	5	7	Studio Lacquer Anti-Scratch	106,660	105,410
B-192	6	3	Satin and Polished Ebony	133,220	131,970
B-192	6	3	Satin and Polished White	135,770	134,520
B-192	6	3	Satin and Polished Ordinary Veneers	150,720	149,470
B-192	6	3	Satin and Polished Special Veneers	152,630	151,380
B-192	6	3	Satin and Polished Extraordinary Veneers	162,940	161,690
B-192 S	6	3	Studio Lacquer Anti-Scratch	123,880	122,630
C-212	7		Satin and Polished Ebony	151,830	150,580
C-212	7		Satin and Polished White	154,330	153,080
C-212	7		Satin and Polished Ordinary Veneers	170,500	169,250
C-212	7		Satin and Polished Special Veneers	172,660	171,410
C-212	7		Satin and Polished Extraordinary Veneers	184,020	182,770
C-212 S	7		Studio Lacquer Anti-Scratch	141,080	139,830
D-232	7	7	Satin and Polished Ebony	178,070	176,820
D-232	7	7	Satin and Polished White	180,510	179,260
D-232	7	7	Satin and Polished Ordinary Veneers	198,040	196,790
D-232	7	7	Satin and Polished Special Veneers	200,310	199,060
D-232	7	7	Satin and Polished Extraordinary Veneers	212,390	211,140
D-232 S	7	7	Studio Lacquer Anti-Scratch	166,020	164,770
E-272	8	11	Satin and Polished Ebony	253,920	252,670

Model	Feet	Inches	Description	MSRP	SMP

STEINGRAEBER & SÖHNE (continued)

Model	Feet	Inches	Description	MSRP	SMP
E-272	8	11	Satin and Polished White	256,420	255,170
E-272	8	11	Satin and Polished Ordinary Veneers	277,720	276,470
E-272	8	11	Satin and Polished Special Veneers	279,590	278,340
E-272	8	11	Satin and Polished Extraordinary Veneers	295,080	293,830

STEINWAY & SONS

These are the prices at the Steinway retail store in New York City, often used as a benchmark for Steinway prices throughout the country. Model K-52 in ebony; model 1098 in ebony, mahogany, and walnut; and grand models in ebony, mahogany, and walnut include adjustable artist benches. Other models include regular wood bench. Wood-veneered models are in a semigloss finish called "satin lustre."

Verticals

Model	Feet	Inches	Description	MSRP	SMP
4510		45	Sheraton Satin Ebony	37,100	37,100
4510		45	Sheraton Mahogany	41,100	41,100
4510		45	Sheraton Walnut	41,600	41,600
1098		46.5	Satin Ebony	35,000	35,000
1098		46.5	Mahogany	38,900	38,900
1098		46.5	Walnut	39,400	39,400
K-52		52	Satin Ebony	40,800	40,800
K-52		52	Mahogany	45,900	45,900
K-52		52	Walnut	47,600	47,600

Grands

Model	Feet	Inches	Description	MSRP	SMP
S	5	1	Satin and Polished Ebony	73,300	73,300
S	5	1	Polished Ebony w/Sterling Hardware	75,300	75,300
S	5	1	Polished White	83,500	83,500
S	5	1	Polished Custom Color	91,900	91,900
S	5	1	Mahogany	89,600	89,600
S	5	1	Walnut	90,600	90,600
S	5	1	Amberwood	95,700	95,700
S	5	1	Applewood	95,700	95,700
S	5	1	Dark Cherry	95,700	95,700
S	5	1	Figured Sapele	95,700	95,700
S	5	1	Figured Sycamore	95,700	95,700
S	5	1	Kewazinga Bubinga	95,700	95,700
S	5	1	Padauk	106,900	106,900
S	5	1	Santos Rosewood	106,900	106,900
S	5	1	East Indian Rosewood	111,000	111,000
S	5	1	Koa	111,000	111,000
S	5	1	African Pommele	112,000	112,000
S	5	1	Macassar Ebony	122,200	122,200
S	5	1	Ziricote	127,100	127,100
M	5	7	Satin and Polished Ebony	78,900	78,900
M	5	7	Polished Ebony w/Sterling Hardware	80,900	80,900
M	5	7	Polished White	89,200	89,200
M	5	7	Polished Custom Color	98,200	98,200
M	5	7	Polished Ebony w/White/Color Pops Accessories	94,400	94,400

Model	Feet	Inches	Description	MSRP	SMP
STEINWAY & SONS (continued)					
M	5	7	Mahogany	95,400	95,400
M	5	7	Walnut	96,500	96,500
M	5	7	Amberwood	101,600	101,600
M	5	7	Applewood	101,600	101,600
M	5	7	Dark Cherry	101,600	101,600
M	5	7	Figured Sapele	101,600	101,600
M	5	7	Figured Sycamore	101,600	101,600
M	5	7	Kewazinga Bubinga	101,600	101,600
M	5	7	Padauk	112,900	112,900
M	5	7	Santos Rosewood	112,900	112,900
M	5	7	Onyx Duet Polished Ebony	115,900	115,900
M	5	7	East Indian Rosewood	117,100	117,100
M	5	7	Koa	117,100	117,100
M	5	7	African Pommele	118,100	118,100
M	5	7	John Lennon Imagine Polished White	122,000	122,000
M	5	7	Macassar Ebony	128,400	128,400
M	5	7	Ziricote	133,400	133,400
M 1014A	5	7	Chippendale Mahogany	109,800	109,800
M 1014A	5	7	Chippendale Walnut	110,800	110,800
M 501A	5	7	Louis XV Walnut	141,400	141,400
M 501A	5	7	Louis XV East Indian Rosewood	161,800	161,800
M Sketch 1111	5	7	The Teague Satin and Polished Ebony (Spirio only, included)	121,600	121,600
M Sketch 1111	5	7	The Teague Walnut (Spirio only, included)	131,600	131,600
M			Spirio Play (playback only) Player Piano System, add	25,000	25,000
M			Spirio | r (playback & record) Player Piano System, add	40,000	40,000
O	5	10.5	Satin and Polished Ebony	87,600	87,600
O	5	10.5	Polished Ebony w/Sterling Hardware	89,600	89,600
O	5	10.5	Polished White	97,800	97,800
O	5	10.5	Polished Custom Color	107,600	107,600
O	5	10.5	Polished Ebony w/White/Color Pops Accessories	102,900	102,900
O	5	10.5	Mahogany	103,900	103,900
O	5	10.5	Walnut	104,900	104,900
O	5	10.5	Amberwood	110,000	110,000
O	5	10.5	Applewood	110,000	110,000
O	5	10.5	Dark Cherry	110,000	110,000
O	5	10.5	Figured Sapele	110,000	110,000
O	5	10.5	Figured Sycamore	110,000	110,000
O	5	10.5	Kewazinga Bubinga	110,000	110,000
O	5	10.5	Padauk	121,200	121,200
O	5	10.5	Santos Rosewood	121,200	121,200
O	5	10.5	Onyx Duet Polished Ebony	125,300	125,300
O	5	10.5	East Indian Rosewood	125,300	125,300
O	5	10.5	Koa	125,300	125,300
O	5	10.5	African Pommele	126,300	126,300
O	5	10.5	John Lennon Imagine Polished White	131,400	131,400

Model	Feet	Inches	Description	MSRP	SMP
STEINWAY & SONS *(continued)*					
O	5	10.5	Macassar Ebony	136,500	136,500
O	5	10.5	Ziricote	141,400	141,400
A	6	2	Satin and Polished Ebony	101,100	101,100
A	6	2	Polished Ebony w/Sterling Hardware	103,100	103,100
A	6	2	Polished White	114,400	114,400
A	6	2	Polished Custom Color	125,900	125,900
A	6	2	Polished Ebony w/White/Color Pops Accessories	118,500	118,500
A	6	2	Mahogany	120,500	120,500
A	6	2	Walnut	121,500	121,500
A	6	2	Amberwood	127,700	127,700
A	6	2	Applewood	127,700	127,700
A	6	2	Dark Cherry	126,600	126,600
A	6	2	Figured Sapele	125,600	125,600
A	6	2	Figured Sycamore	127,700	127,700
A	6	2	Kewazinga Bubinga	127,700	127,700
A	6	2	Padauk	140,900	140,900
A	6	2	Santos Rosewood	140,900	140,900
A	6	2	Onyx Duet Polished Ebony	138,900	138,900
A	6	2	East Indian Rosewood	145,000	145,000
A	6	2	Koa	145,000	145,000
A	6	2	African Pommele	149,100	149,100
A	6	2	John Lennon Imagine Polished White	154,200	154,200
A	6	2	Macassar Ebony	158,300	158,300
A	6	2	Ziricote	164,100	164,100
B	6	11	Satin and Polished Ebony	114,300	114,300
B	6	11	Polished Ebony w/Sterling Hardware	118,300	118,300
B	6	11	Polished White	127,500	127,500
B	6	11	Polished Custom Color	140,300	140,300
B	6	11	Polished Ebony w/White/Color Pops Accessories	131,600	131,600
B	6	11	Mahogany	133,700	133,700
B	6	11	Walnut	134,700	134,700
B	6	11	Amberwood	140,800	140,800
B	6	11	Applewood	140,800	140,800
B	6	11	Dark Cherry	139,800	139,800
B	6	11	Figured Sapele	138,800	138,800
B	6	11	Figured Sycamore	140,800	140,800
B	6	11	Kewazinga Bubinga	140,800	140,800
B	6	11	Padauk	154,100	154,100
B	6	11	Santos Rosewood	154,100	154,100
B	6	11	Onyx Duet Polished Ebony	152,000	152,000
B	6	11	East Indian Rosewood	158,100	158,100
B	6	11	Koa	158,100	158,100
B	6	11	African Pommele	162,200	162,200
B	6	11	John Lennon Imagine Polished White	167,300	167,300
B	6	11	Macassar Ebony	171,400	171,400
B	6	11	Ziricote	177,200	177,200

Model	Feet	Inches	Description	MSRP	SMP
STEINWAY & SONS *(continued)*					
B	6	11	Black Diamond Ebony (Spirio | r only, included)	275,000	275,000
B	6	10.5	Black Diamond Macassar Ebony (Spirio | r only, included)	375,000	375,000
B			Spirio Play (playback only) Player Piano System, add	25,000	25,000
B			Spirio | r (playback & record) Player Piano System, add	40,000	40,000
D	8	11.75	Satin and Polished Ebony	181,600	181,600
D	8	11.75	Polished Ebony w/Sterling Hardware	185,600	185,600
D	8	11.75	Polished White	200,200	200,200
D	8	11.75	Polished Custom Color	220,300	220,300
D	8	11.75	Polished Ebony w/White/Color Pops Accessories	202,200	202,200
D	8	11.75	Mahogany	212,500	212,500
D	8	11.75	Walnut	213,600	213,600
D	8	11.75	Amberwood	223,900	223,900
D	8	11.75	Applewood	223,900	223,900
D	8	11.75	Dark Cherry	220,800	220,800
D	8	11.75	Figured Sapele	217,700	217,700
D	8	11.75	Figured Sycamore	223,900	223,900
D	8	11.75	Kewazinga Bubinga	223,900	223,900
D	8	11.75	Padauk	240,300	240,300
D	8	11.75	Santos Rosewood	240,300	240,300
D	8	11.75	East Indian Rosewood	254,800	254,800
D	8	11.75	Koa	254,800	254,800
D	8	11.75	African Pommele	266,100	266,100
D	8	11.75	John Lennon Imagine Polished White	235,200	235,200
D	8	11.75	Macassar Ebony	275,400	275,400
D	8	11.75	Ziricote	284,800	284,800
D	8	11.75	Black Diamond Macassar Ebony (Spirio | r only, included)	585,000	585,000
D	8	11.75	Spirio | *r* (playback & record) Player Piano System, add	40,000	40,000

Steinway (Hamburg) Grands

I requently get requests for prices of pianos made in Steinway's branch factory in Hamburg, Germany. Officially, these pianos are not sold in North America, but it is possible to order one through an American Steinway dealer, or to go to Europe and purchase one there. The following list shows approximately how much it would cost to purchase a Hamburg Steinway in Europe and have it shipped to the United States. The list was derived by taking the published retail price in Europe, subtracting the value-added tax not applicable to foreign purchasers, converting to U.S. dollars (the rate used here is 1 Euro = $1.10, but is obviously subject to change), and adding approximate charges for duty, air freight, crating, insurance, brokerage fees, and delivery. Only prices for grands in polished ebony are shown here. Caution: This list is published for general informational purposes only. The price that Steinway would charge for a piano ordered through an American Steinway dealer may be different. (Also, the cost of a trip to Europe to purchase the piano is not included.)

Model	Feet	Inches	Description	MSRP	SMP
S-155	5	1	Polished Ebony	84,300	84,300
M-170	5	7	Polished Ebony	87,200	87,200
O-180	5	10.5	Polished Ebony	95,900	95,900
A-188	6	2	Polished Ebony	98,400	98,400
B-211	6	11	Polished Ebony	113,350	113,350
C-227	7	5.5	Polished Ebony	127,400	127,400
D-274	8	11.75	Polished Ebony	170,700	170,700

Model	Feet	Inches	Description	MSRP	SMP

STORY & CLARK

All Story & Clark pianos include PNOscan, and USB and MIDI connectivity. In addition, all grands now include a QRS PNOmation player-piano system. Prices shown are those for online sales through **www.qrsmusic.com**.

Heritage Series Verticals

Model	Feet	Inches	Description	MSRP	SMP
H7		46	Academy Polished Ebony		5,395

Signature Series Verticals

Model	Feet	Inches	Description	MSRP	SMP
S8		48	Cosmopolitan Polished Ebony		5,395

Heritage Series Grands

Model	Feet	Inches	Description	MSRP	SMP
H50A	4	11	Prelude Polished Ebony/Mahogany		16,695
H60 QA	5		French Provincial Polished Ebony		17,495
H60 QA	5		French Provincial Satin Lacquer and Polished Mahogany		17,595
H60A	5	3	Academy Satin and Polished Ebony		17,495
H60A	5	3	Academy Polished Mahogany		17,495
H60A	5	3	Academy Polished White		17,995
H70A	5	7	Conservatory Polished Ebony		18,895
H80	6	1	Professional Polished Ebony		21,395
H90	6	10	Semi-Concert Polished Ebony		28,795

Signature Series Grands

Model	Feet	Inches	Description	MSRP	SMP
S500	4	11	Manhattan Semigloss Ebony w/Birdseye Maple Accents		25,095
S600	5	4	Cosmopolitan Polished Ebony		24,395
S600	5	4	Melrose Polished Ebony/Mahogany		26,995
S600	5	4	Park West Satin Ebony		24,195
S600	5	4	Park West Polished Ebony		24,495
S700	5	9	Fairfax Polished Ebony w/Bubinga Accents		26,695
S700	5	9	Versailles Satin Lacquer Cherry		26,295
S700	5	9	Park West Polished Ebony		24,695
S800	6	2	Islander British Colonial Satin Walnut		27,895
S800	6	2	Park West Polished Ebony		25,395
S900	7		Park West Satin Ebony		38,495

WALTER, CHARLES R.

Verticals

Model	Feet	Inches	Description	MSRP	SMP
1520		43	Satin and Polished Walnut		20,150
1520		43	Satin and Polished Cherry		20,088
1520		43	Satin and Polished Oak		19,442
1520		43	Satin and Polished Mahogany		20,502
1520		43	Italian Provincial Satin and Polished Walnut		20,388
1520		43	Italian Provincial Satin and Polished Mahogany		20,542
1520		43	Italian Provincial Satin and Polished Oak		19,884
1520		43	Country Classic Satin and Polished Cherry		19,914
1520		43	Country Classic Satin and Polished Oak		19,576
1520		43	French Provincial Satin and Polished Oak		20,188
1520		43	French Provincial Satin and Polished Cherry/Walnut/Mahogany		20,776

Model	Feet	Inches	Description	MSRP	SMP

WALTER, CHARLES R. *(continued)*

Model	Feet	Inches	Description	MSRP	SMP
1520		43	Riviera Satin and Polished Oak		19,588
1520		43	Queen Anne Satin and Polished Oak		20,348
1520		43	Queen Anne Satin and Polished Mahogany/Cherry		20,776
1500		45	Satin Ebony		18,778
1500		45	Semi-Gloss Ebony		19,130
1500		45	Polished Ebony (Lacquer)		19,342
1500		45	Polished Ebony (Polyester)		19,736
1500		45	Satin and Polished Oak		18,390
1500		45	Satin and Polished Walnut		18,976
1500		45	Satin and Polished Mahogany		19,248
1500		45	Satin and Polished Gothic Oak		18,996
1500		45	Satin and Polished Cherry		19,388
Verticals			Renner (German) action, add		1,500

Grands

Model	Feet	Inches	Description	MSRP	SMP
W-175	5	9	Satin Ebony		82,758
W-175	5	9	Semi-Polished Ebony		84,622
W-175	5	9	Polished Ebony (Lacquer)		86,622
W-175	5	9	Polished Ebony (Polyester)		88,622
W-175	5	9	Satin Mahogany/Walnut/Cherry		89,400
W-175	5	9	Semi-Polished Mahogany/Walnut/Cherry		90,600
W-175	5	9	Polished Mahogany/Walnut/Cherry		91,000
W-175	5	9	Open-Pore Walnut		87,400
W-175	5	9	Satin Oak		79,940
W-175	5	9	Chippendale Satin Mahogany/Cherry		93,400
W-175	5	9	Chippendale Semi-Polished Mahogany/Cherry		93,800
W-175	5	9	Chippendale Polished Mahogany/Cherry		94,200
W-190	6	4	Satin Ebony		87,000
W-190	6	4	Semi-Polished Ebony		88,000
W-190	6	4	Polished Ebony (Lacquer)		90,000
W-190	6	4	Polished Ebony (Polyester)		92,000
W-190	6	4	Satin Mahogany/Walnut/Cherry		92,800
W-190	6	4	Semi-Polished Mahogany/Walnut/Cherry		94,000
W-190	6	4	Polished Mahogany/Walnut/Cherry		94,400
W-190	6	4	Open-Pore Walnut		90,800
W-190	6	4	Satin Oak		84,940
W-190	6	4	Chippendale Satin Mahogany/Cherry		97,400
W-190	6	4	Chippendale Semi-Polished Mahogany/Cherry		97,800
W-190	6	4	Chippendale Polished Mahogany/Cherry		98,200

WEBER

Weber Verticals

Model	Feet	Inches	Description	MSRP	SMP
W114		45	Polished Ebony	6,390	6,080
W114		45	Polished Mahogany	6,690	6,280
W121		48	Polished Ebony	7,190	6,780

Model	Feet	Inches	Description	MSRP	SMP
WEBER *(continued)*					
W121		48	Polished Mahogany/Walnut/White	7,490	6,980
W131		52	Polished Ebony	7,890	7,180
W131		52	Polished Mahogany	7,990	7,780
Albert Weber Verticals					
AW 121		48	Polished Ebony	11,890	9,980
AW 121		48	Satin Mahogany	11,990	10,380
AW 121E		48	Polished Ebony w/Chrome	12,790	10,980
AW 131		52	Satin Ebony	14,200	12,780
AW 131		52	Polished Ebony	14,090	11,980
Weber Grands					
W150	4	11	Polished Ebony	14,490	12,580
W150	4	11	Polished Mahogany/Walnut/White	14,790	12,980
W150SP	4	11	Polished Ebony w/Chrome	15,190	13,180
W150SP	4	11	Polished White w/Chrome	15,290	13,380
W157	5	2	Polished Ebony	15,490	13,380
W157	5	2	Polished Mahogany	15,990	13,980
W175	5	9	Polished Ebony	17,490	14,780
W185	6	1	Polished Ebony	21,490	17,780
Albert Weber Grands					
AW 185	6	1	Polished Ebony	37,550	30,180
AW 208	6	10	Polished Ebony	46,350	36,780
AW 228	7	6	Polished Ebony	64,390	50,780
AW 275	9		Polished Ebony	116,190	88,780

WENDL & LUNG

Model	Feet	Inches	Description	MSRP	SMP
Verticals					
120		47	Polished Ebony	11,985	6,990
120		47	Polished Mahogany/Walnut	12,785	7,390
126		49.6	Polished Ebony	16,620	10,080
126		49.6	Polished Mahogany/Walnut	17,348	10,480
130		51	Polished Ebony	17,460	10,640
130		51	Polished Mahogany/Walnut	18,182	11,040
Grands					
152	5		Polished Ebony	25,920	16,280
152	5		Polished Mahogany/Walnut	27,595	17,280
162	5	4	Polished Ebony	31,170	19,780
162	5	4	Polished Mahogany/Walnut	32,835	20,780
180	5	11	Polished Ebony	35,922	22,948
180	5	11	Polished Mahogany/Walnut	37,554	23,948

Model	Feet	Inches	Description	MSRP	SMP
WERTHEIM					
Verticals					
W121L		48	Polished Ebony	6,499	5,999
W123		48.5	Polished Ebony	6,999	6,499
W123		48.5	Polished Mahogany	7,299	6,999
WE123		48.5	Polished Ebony	8,999	8,499
WF125V1		49	Polished Ebony	17,999	16,999
WF125V3		49	Polished Ebony	11,999	11,299
W126		49.5	Polished Ebony	7,299	6,999
Grands					
W160	5	3	Polished Ebony	12,499	10,999
W160	5	3	Polished Mahogany	13,499	11,999
WF165	5	5	Polished Ebony	29,999	24,999
WE170	5	7	Polished Ebony	18,999	15,999
WE170	5	7	Polished Mahogany	19,999	14,999
WP180	5	11	Polished Ebony	29,999	24,999

YAMAHA
Including Disklavier, Silent, and TransAcoustic Pianos

Model	Feet	Inches	Description	MSRP	SMP
Verticals					
b1		43	Continental Polished Ebony	4,799	4,799
b1		43	Continental Polished Ebony with Chrome Accents	4,999	4,999
b1		43	Continental Polished White	4,999	4,999
M560		44	Hancock Satin Brown Cherry	7,899	7,899
b2		45	Polished Ebony	6,749	6,598
b2		45	Polished Ebony with Chrome Accents	6,949	6,798
b2		45	Polished Mahogany/Walnut/White	7,159	6,998
P22D		45	Satin Ebony	7,849	7,598
P22D		45	Satin Walnut/Dark Oak	8,199	7,998
P660		45	Sheraton Satin Brown Mahogany	9,979	9,979
P660		45	Queen Anne Satin Brown Cherry	9,979	9,979
b3		48	Polished Ebony	8,259	7,798
b3		48	Polished Ebony with Chrome Accents	8,459	7,998
b3		48	Polished Mahogany/Walnut/White	9,129	8,298
U1		48	Satin and Polished Ebony	11,399	11,399
U1		48	Satin American Walnut	13,499	13,499
U1		48	Polished Mahogany/White	13,499	13,499
YUS1		48	Satin and Polished Ebony	15,599	14,998
YUS1		48	Satin American Walnut	18,799	17,930
YUS1		48	Polished Mahogany/White	18,799	17,930
U3		52	Polished Ebony	14,559	14,098
U3		52	Satin American Walnut	16,599	16,398
U3		52	Polished Mahogany	16,599	16,398
YUS3		52	Polished Ebony	18,899	17,998

Model	Feet	Inches	Description	MSRP	SMP
YAMAHA *(continued)*					
YUS3		52	Polished Mahogany	21,799	20,598
YUS5		52	Polished Ebony	20,999	19,978
SU7		52	Polished Ebony	39,999	38,390
Disklavier Verticals					
DU1ENST		48	Satin and Polished Ebony	29,099	27,558
DU1ENST		48	Satin American Walnut	31,199	29,698
DU1ENST		48	Polished Mahogany/White	31,199	29,698
DYUS1ENST		48	Satin and Polished Ebony	33,299	30,698
DYUS1ENST		48	Satin American Walnut	36,499	33,630
DYUS1ENST		48	Polished Mahogany/White	36,499	33,630
DYUS5ENST		52	Polished Ebony	38,699	35,678
Silent and TransAcoustic Verticals					
b1SC2		43	Polished Ebony	9,299	9,398
b1SC2		43	Polished Ebony with Chrome Accents	9,499	9,698
b1SC2		43	Polished White	9,499	9,698
b2SC2		45	Polished Ebony	11,249	10,298
b2SC2		45	Polished Ebony with Chrome Accents	11,449	10,498
b2SC2		45	Polished Mahogany/Walnut/White	11,659	10,698
P22DSC2		45	Satin Ebony	12,349	11,298
P22DSC2		45	Satin Walnut/Dark Oak	12,699	11,698
b3SC2		48	Polished Ebony	12,759	11,498
b3SC2		48	Polished Ebony with Chrome Accents	12,959	11,698
b3SC2		48	Polished Mahogany/Walnut/White	13,629	11,998
U1SH2		48	Satin and Polished Ebony	15,899	15,558
U1SH2		48	Satin American Walnut	17,999	17,698
U1SH2		48	Polished Mahogany/White	17,999	17,698
U1TA2		48	Polished Ebony	17,899	17,558
YUS1SH2		48	Satin and Polished Ebony	20,099	18,698
YUS1SH2		48	Satin American Walnut	23,299	21,630
YUS1SH2		48	Polished Mahogany/White	23,299	21,630
YUS1TA2		48	Polished Ebony	22,099	20,698
U3SH2		52	Polished Ebony	19,059	17,798
U3SH2		52	Polished Mahogany	21,099	20,098
U3SH2		52	Satin American Walnut	21,099	20,098
YUS3SH2		52	Polished Ebony	23,399	21,698
YUS3SH2		52	Polished Mahogany	26,299	24,298
YUS3TA2		52	Polished Ebony	25,399	23,698
YUS5SH2		52	Polished Ebony	25,499	23,678
YUS5TA2		52	Polished Ebony	27,499	15,678
Grands					
GB1K	5		Polished Ebony	14,999	14,158
GB1K	5		Polished American Walnut/Mahogany/White	17,339	16,198
GB1K	5		French Provincial Satin Cherry	19,179	18,598
GB1K	5		Georgian Satin Mahogany	18,359	18,198

Model	Feet	Inches	Description	MSRP	SMP
YAMAHA *(continued)*					
GC1M	5	3	Satin and Polished Ebony	23,999	23,858
GC1M	5	3	Satin American Walnut	30,599	28,198
GC1M	5	3	Polished Mahogany/White	30,599	28,198
C1X	5	3	Satin and Polished Ebony	37,999	34,098
C1X	5	3	Satin American Walnut	46,369	41,118
C1X	5	3	Polished Mahogany/White	46,369	41,118
GC2	5	8	Satin and Polished Ebony	28,959	26,998
GC2	5	8	Satin American Walnut	33,859	31,198
GC2	5	8	Polished Mahogany/White	33,859	31,198
C2X	5	8	Satin and Polished Ebony	43,999	40,198
C2X	5	8	Polished Ebony w/Chrome Accents	45,699	41,398
C2X	5	8	Satin American Walnut	53,399	47,938
C2X	5	8	Polished Mahogany/White	53,399	47,938
C3X	6	1	Satin and Polished Ebony	57,999	52,298
C3X	6	1	Satin American Walnut	69,999	62,798
C3X	6	1	Polished Mahogany/White	69,999	62,798
S3X	6	1	Polished Ebony	77,999	74,998
CF4	6	3	Polished Ebony	105,599	105,599
C5X	6	7	Satin and Polished Ebony	63,899	58,098
C5X	6	7	Satin American Walnut	77,799	69,560
C5X	6	7	Polished Mahogany/White	77,799	69,560
S5X	6	7	Polished Ebony	84,999	80,998
C6X	7		Satin and Polished Ebony	71,199	64,698
C6X	7		Satin American Walnut	85,999	77,718
C6X	7		Polished Mahogany/White	85,999	77,718
S6X	7		Polished Ebony	95,599	92,998
CF6	7		Polished Ebony	119,999	119,598
C7X	7	6	Satin and Polished Ebony	82,999	74,698
C7X	7	6	Satin American Walnut	99,999	89,478
C7X	7	6	Polished Mahogany/White	99,999	89,478
S7X	7	6	Polished Ebony	104,999	100,998
CFX	9		Polished Ebony	179,999	179,999
C7X	7	6	Satin American Walnut	99,999	89,478
C7X	7	6	Polished Mahogany/White	99,999	89,478
S7X	7	6	Polished Ebony	104,999	100,998
CFX	9		Polished Ebony	179,999	179,999
Disklavier Grands					
DGB1KENCL	5		Classic Polished Ebony (playback only)	23,999	23,158
DGB1KENST	5		Polished Ebony	28,599	26,758
DGB1KENST	5		Polished Mahogany/American Walnut/White	30,939	28,798
DGC1ENST	5	3	Satin and Polished Ebony	41,699	39,558
DGC1ENST	5	3	Satin American Walnut	48,299	43,898
DGC1ENST	5	3	Polished Mahogany/White	48,299	43,898

Model	Feet	Inches	Description	MSRP	SMP
YAMAHA *(continued)*					
DC1XENST	5	3	Satin and Polished Ebony	55,699	49,798
DC1XENST	5	3	Satin American Walnut	64,069	56,818
DC1XENST	5	3	Polished Mahogany/White	64,069	56,818
DGC2ENST	5	8	Satin and Polished Ebony	46,659	42,698
DGC2ENST	5	8	Satin American Walnut	51,559	46,898
DGC2ENST	5	8	Polished Mahogany/White	51,559	46,898
DC2XENST	5	8	Satin and Polished Ebony	61,699	55,898
DC2XENST	5	8	Polished Ebony w/Chrome Accents	63,399	57,098
DC2XENST	5	8	Satin American Walnut	71,099	63,638
DC2XENST	5	8	Polished Mahogany/White	71,099	63,638
DC3XENPRO	6	1	Satin and Polished Ebony	80,899	71,098
DC3XENPRO	6	1	Satin American Walnut	92,899	81,598
DC3XENPRO	6	1	Polished Mahogany/White	92,899	81,598
DS3XENPRO	6	1	Polished Ebony	117,999	112,998
DCF4ENPRO	6	3	Polished Ebony	145,599	144,198
DC5XENPRO	6	7	Satin and Polished Ebony	86,799	76,898
DC5XENPRO	6	7	Satin American Walnut	100,699	88,360
DC5XENPRO	6	7	Polished Mahogany/White	100,699	88,360
DS5XENPRO	6	7	Polished Ebony	124,999	118,998
DC6XENPRO	7		Satin and Polished Ebony	94,099	83,498
DC6XENPRO	7		Satin American Walnut	108,899	96,518
DC6XENPRO	7		Polished Mahogany/White	108,899	96,518
DS6XENPRO	7		Polished Ebony	135,599	130,998
DCF6ENPRO	7		Polished Ebony	159,999	157,598
DC7XENPRO	7	6	Satin and Polished Ebony	105,899	93,498
DC7XENPRO	7	6	Satin American Walnut	122,899	108,278
DC7XENPRO	7	6	Polished Mahogany/White	122,899	108,278
DS7XEMPRO	7	6	Polished Ebony	144,999	138,998
DCFXENPRO	9		Polished Ebony	219,999	218,998
Silent and TransAcoustic Grands					
GB1KSC2	5		Polished Ebony	19,499	17,858
GB1KSC2	5		Polished Mahogany/Walnut/White	21,839	19,898
GC1SH2	5	3	Satin and Polished Ebony	28,499	27,558
GC1SH2	5	3	Satin American Walnut	35,099	31,898
GC1SH2	5	3	Polished Mahogany/White	35,099	31,898
GC1TA2	5	3	Polished Ebony	32,499	31,558
C1XSH2	5	3	Satin and Polished Ebony	42,499	37,798
C1XSH2	5	3	Satin American Walnut	50,869	44,818
C1XSH2	5	3	Polished Mahogany/White	50,869	44,818
C1XTA2	5	3	Polished Ebony	46,499	41,798
GC2SH2	5	8	Satin and Polished Ebony	33,459	30,698
GC2SH2	5	8	Satin American Walnut	38,359	34,898
GC2SH2	5	8	Polished Mahogany/White	38,359	34,898
C2XSH2	5	8	Satin and Polished Ebony	48,499	43,898

PIANOBUYER *Model & Price Supplement*

Model	Feet	Inches	Description	MSRP	SMP
YAMAHA *(continued)*					
C2XSH2	5	8	Polished Ebony w/Chrome Accents	50,199	45,098
C2XSH2	5	8	Satin American Walnut	57,899	51,638
C2XSH2	5	8	Polished Mahogany/White	57,899	51,638
C3XSH2	6	1	Satin and Polished Ebony	62,499	55,998
C3XSH2	6	1	Satin American Walnut	74,499	66,498
C3XSH2	6	1	Polished Mahogany/White	74,499	66,498
C3XTA2	6	1	Polished Ebony	66,499	59,998
C5XSH2	6	7	Satin and Polished Ebony	68,399	61,798
C5XSH2	6	7	Satin American Walnut	82,299	73,260
C5XSH2	6	7	Polished Mahogany/White	82,299	73,260
C6XSH2	7		Satin and Polished Ebony	75,699	68,398
C6XSH2	7		Satin American Walnut	90,499	81,418
C6XSH2	7		Polished Mahogany/White	90,499	81,418
C7XSH2	7	6	Satin and Polished Ebony	87,499	78,398
C7XSH2	7	6	Satin American Walnut	104,499	93,178
C7XSH2	7	6	Polished Mahogany/White	104,499	93,178

YOUNG CHANG

Verticals

Model		Inches	Description	MSRP	SMP
Y114		45	Polished Ebony	5,990	5,900
Y114		45	Polished Mahogany	6,450	6,100
Y116		46	Polished Ebony	7,490	6,900
Y116		46	Satin Ebony/Walnut	7,590	7,000
Y121		48	Polished Ebony	7,090	6,500
Y121		48	Polished Mahogany/White	7,090	6,700
Y131		52	Polished Ebony	7,590	6,900
Y131		52	Polished Mahogany	7,790	7,100

Grands

Model	Feet	Inches	Description	MSRP	SMP
Y150	4	11	Polished Ebony	13,290	11,580
Y150	4	11	Polished Mahogany/Walnut/White	13,790	11,980
Y150SP	4	11	Polished White w/Chrome	14,090	12,780
Y157	5	2	Polished Ebony	14,390	12,780
Y157	5	2	Polished Mahogany	14,990	13,380
Y175	5	9	Polished Ebony	16,390	14,180
Y185	6	1	Polished Ebony	20,390	17,180

ZIMMERMANN

Verticals

Model		Inches	Description	MSRP	SMP
S 2		47.6	Polished Ebony	8,590	8,440
S 6		49.6	Polished Ebony	9,590	9,166

Model	Feet	Inches	Description	MSRP	SMP
ZIMMERMANN (continued)					
Grands					
Z 160	5	3	Polished Ebony	20,900	20,397
Z 175	5	9	Polished Ebony	22,900	22,848
Z 185	6	1	Polished Ebony	24,900	24,299

Digital Piano
Specifications & Prices

In the specification chart for each brand of digital piano, we have included those features and specifications about which buyers, in our experience, are most likely to be curious. However, many models have more features than are shown. See the various articles on digital pianos on our website for more information about each of the terms defined below, shown in the order in which they appear in the charts.

Form The physical form of the model: G=Grand, V= Vertical (Console), S=Slab.

Ensemble A digital piano with easy-play and auto-accompaniments (not just rhythms).

Finish The wood finishes or colors available for a particular model (not always specified for slab models). Multiple finish options are separated by a slash (/). A manufacturer's own color term is used where a generic term could not be determined. See the box below for finish codes.

FINISH CODES			
A	Ash	**O**	Oak
AG	Amber Glow	**Or**	Orange
Al	Alder	**P**	Polished (used with a wood or color designation)
Bl	Blue		
Bk	Black	**Pk**	Pink
C	Cherry	**R**	Rosewood
DB	Deep Brunette	**Rd**	Red
E	Ebony	**S**	Satin (used with a wood or color designation)
G	Gold		
Iv	Ivory	**Sr**	Silver
L	Lacquer (used with a wood or color designation)	**VR**	Velvette Rouge
		W	Walnut
M	Mahogany	**WG**	Wood Grain (wood type not specified)
MD	Mahogany Decor	**Wt**	White

Estimated Price This is our estimate of the price you will pay for the instrument. For digitals sold online or through chain and warehouse outlets, this price is the Minimum Advertised Price (MAP) and is shown in italics. For digitals sold only through bricks-and-mortar piano dealers, the price shown is based on a profit margin that piano dealers typically aspire to when selling digitals, including an allowance for incoming freight and setup. Discounts from this price, if any, typically are small. For more information on MAP and other pricing issues, please read "Buying a Digital Piano," elsewhere in this issue.

MSRP Manufacturer's Suggested Retail Price, also known as "list" or "sticker" price. Not all manufacturers use them.

Sound Source Indicates whether the sound source is Sampling (S) or Physical Modeling (M).

Voices The number of different musical voices the user can select from the instrument panel, plus (if applicable) the number of General MIDI (GM) or XG voices that are not user-selectable but are available for playback of MIDI files.

Key Off Indicates the presence of samples or simulation of Key Off sounds—acoustic piano keys and dampers returning to rest position and cutting off the sounds of vibrating strings.

Sustain Indicates the presence of samples or simulation of the sound with the sustain pedal depressed (allowing the strings to vibrate sympathetically).

String Resonance Indicates the presence of samples or simulation of String Resonance—the resonance sound of the strings of non-played notes.

Rhythms/Styles The number of rhythms in a standard digital, or the number of auto-accompaniment styles available in an ensemble digital.

Polyphony The maximum number of sounds the instrument can produce simultaneously. UL=Unlimited

Total Watts Total combined amplifier power.

Speakers The number of individual speakers.

Piano Pedals The number of piano pedals supplied with the model. A number in parentheses indicates the availability of an optional pedal unit with additional pedals.

Half Pedal Indicates that the model supports half-pedaling.

Action Indicates the type of action used, if specified.

Triple-Sensor Keys Indicates the presence of three key sensors, instead of the usual two, for greater touch realism.

Escapement Indicates the presence of an acoustic piano action's escapement feel.

Wood Keys Indicates actions with wooden keys.

Ivory Texture Indicates actions with ivory-textured keytops.

Bluetooth Indicates that the instrument is equipped with Bluetooth for connecting to theInternet.

Vocal Support The model supports some level of vocal performance. This support can vary from the piano simply having a microphone input, to its having the ability to produce the vocalist's voice in multi-part harmony, to pitch-correct the notes sung by the vocalist, or to alter the original voice.

Educational Features The model includes features that specifically support the learning experience. Note that while the ability to record and play back is an important learning tool, it is present on almost all models and so is not included in this definition.

External Storage Indicates the type of external memory storage accessible, such as USB or SanDisk.

USB to Computer Indicates the model's ability to interface with a Mac or PC via USB cable.

USB Digital Audio Indicates the ability to record and play back digital audio via a USB flash drive.

Recording Tracks The number of internal recordable tracks for recording of MIDI files.

Warranty (Parts/Labor) Indicates the manufacturer's warranty coverage period: the first number is the length of the parts coverage; the second number is the length of the labor coverage.

Dimensions Width, Depth, and Height are rounded to the nearest inch.

Weight Weight of the model rounded to the nearest pound.

Brand & Model	Form	Ensemble	Finish	Estimated Price	MSRP	Sound Source	Voices	Key Off	Sustain	String Resonance	Rhythms/Styles	Polyphony	Total Watts	Speakers	Piano Pedals	Half Pedal
Artesia																
Performer	S		Bk	*200*		S	12	Y	Y			32	15	4	1	Y
PA-88H	S		Bk/Wt	*379*		S	16	Y	Y			64	20	2	1	Y
PE-88	S		Bk	*299*		S	137	Y	Y	100		64	15	4	1 (2)	Y
Harmony	V		Bk	*495*		S	16	Y	Y			64	20	2	3	Y
DP-2	V		R	*599*		S	8	Y	Y			64	25	4	2	Y
DP-3	V		R	*699*		S	8	Y	Y			64	25	2	3	Y
DP-150e	V	E	EP/R	*850*		S	137	Y	Y	100		64	40	4	3	Y
AG-30	G	E	EP	*1,499*		S	137	Y	Y	100		128	60	6	3	Y
AG-50	G	E	EP	*2,399*		S	137	Y	Y	100		128	75	6	3	Y
Blüthner																
e-Klavier PRO-88 EX	S		ESL	2,736	3,326	S	35+ 256GM	Y	Y	Y		256	60	2	3 (5)	Y
e-Klavier 2	V		ESL/WtSL	5,704	6,381	S	35+ 256GM	Y	Y	Y		256	100	4	3	Y
e-Klavier 2	V		EPL	6,534	7,389	S	35+ 256GM	Y	Y	Y		256	100	4	3	Y
e-Klavier 3	V		ESL/WtSL	6,508	7,358	S	25+ 127GM	Y	Y	Y		256	150	4	3	Y
e-Klavier 3	V		EPL	7,337	8,366	S	25+ 127GM	Y	Y	Y		256	150	4	3	Y
e-Klavier Pianette	V		EPL	15,907	18,782	S	35+ 256GM	Y	Y	Y		256	150	4	3	Y
e-Klavier Homeline	V		ES	4,322	4,701	S	35+ 256GM	Y	Y	Y		256	60	4	3	Y
e-Klavier Homeline	V		Stained wood	4,599	5,037	S	35+ 256GM	Y	Y	Y		256	60	4	3	Y
e-Klavier Homeline	V		Waxed beechwood	4,875	5,373	S	35+ 256GM	Y	Y	Y		256	60	4	3	Y
e-Grand Studio	G		ESL/WtSL	11,279	12,936	S	35+ 256GM	Y	Y	Y		256	150	4	3	Y
e-Grand Studio	G		EPL/WtPL	13,767	15,960	S	35+ 256GM	Y	Y	Y		256	150	4	3	Y
e-Grand Concert	G		ESL/WtSL	15,978	18,648	S	35+ 256GM	Y	Y	Y		256	150	6	3	Y
e-Grand Concert	G		EPL/WtPL	19,261	22,638	S	35+ 256GM	Y	Y	Y		256	150	6	3	Y
Casio																
PX-5S	S		Wt	*999*	1,399	S	242+ 128GM	Y	Y	Y		256	0	0	1 (2)	
PX-160	S		Bk/G	*549*	849	S	18		Y			128	16	2	1 (3)	Y
PX-360	S	E	Bk	*899*	1,199	S	422+ 128GM	Y	Y	Y	200	128	16	4	1 (3)	Y

Brand & Model	Action	Triple-Sensor Keys	Escapement	Wood Keys	Ivory Texture	Bluetooth	Vocal Support	Educational Features	External Storage	USB to Computer	USB Digital Audio	Recording Tracks	Warranty (Parts/Labor)	Dimensions WxDxH (Inches)	Weight (Pounds)
Artesia															
Performer	Soft Touch Spring Tension	Y			Y				USB	Y	Y	0	1/3	50x11x3	22
PA-88H	Weighted Hammer Action	Y			Y				USB	Y	Y	0	1/3	52x14x5	29
PE-88	Semi-Weighted Spring Action	Y			Y			Y	USB	Y	Y	2	1/3	55x13x7	27
Harmony	Weighted Hammer Action	Y			Y				USB	Y	Y	0	1/3	58x20x9	48
DP-2	Graded Hammer Action	Y			Y			Y	USB	Y	Y	2	3/3	54x40x17	132
DP-3	Graded Hammer Action	Y			Y			Y	USB	Y	Y	2	3/3	59x22x14	132
DP-150e	Graded Hammer Action	Y			Y	Y		Y	USB	Y	Y	2	3/3	59x25x15	154
AG-30	Graded Hammer Action	Y			Y	Y		Y	USB	Y	Y	2	3/3	56x33x36	170
AG-50	Graded Hammer Action	Y			Y	Y		Y	USB	Y	Y	2	3/3	56x48x36	240
Blüthner															
e-Klavier PRO-88 EX	4-zone graded				Y	Y			USB	Y	Y	1	2	55x17x5	30
e-Klavier 2	4-zone graded			Y	Y	Y			USB	Y	Y	1	2	55x25x42	220
e-Klavier 2	4-zone graded			Y	Y	Y			USB	Y	Y	1	2	55x25x42	220
e-Klavier 3	4-zone graded			Y	Y	Y			USB	Y	Y	1	2	55x25x42	230
e-Klavier 3	4-zone graded			Y	Y	Y			USB	Y	Y	1	2	55x25x42	230
e-Klavier Pianette	4-zone graded			Y	Y	Y			USB	Y	Y	1	2	55x25x42	220
e-Klavier Homeline	4-zone graded		Y			Y			USB	Y	Y	1	2	140x60x35	135
e-Klavier Homeline	4-zone graded		Y			Y			USB	Y	Y	1	2	140x60x35	135
e-Klavier Homeline	4-zone graded		Y			Y			USB	Y	Y	1	2	140x60x35	135
e-Grand Studio	4-zone graded			Y	Y	Y			USB	Y	Y	1	2	51x33x35	225
e-Grand Studio	4-zone graded			Y	Y	Y			USB	Y	Y	1	2	51x33x35	225
e-Grand Concert	4-zone graded			Y	Y	Y			USB	Y	Y	1	2	51x55x35	248
e-Grand Concert	4-zone graded			Y	Y	Y			USB	Y	Y	1	2	51x55x35	248
Casio															
PX-5S	Weighted, Scaled, Hammer Action	Y			Y				USB	Y	Y	8	3/3	52x11x5	24
PX-160	Weighted, Scaled, Hammer Action	Y			Y		Y			Y		2	3/3	52x12x6	26
PX-360	Weighted, Scaled, Hammer Action	Y			Y			Y	USB	Y	Y	17	3/3	52x12x6	26

Casio (continued)

Brand & Model	Form	Ensemble	Finish	Estimated Price	MSRP	Sound Source	Voices	Key Off	Sustain	String Resonance	Rhythms/Styles	Polyphony	Total Watts	Speakers	Piano Pedals	Half Pedal
PX-560	S	E	Bl	1,199	1,599	S	522+ 128GM	Y	Y	Y	230	256	16	4	1 (3)	Y
PX-770	V		Bk/W/Wt	749	1,149	S	19		Y			128	16	2	3	Y
PX-780	V	E	Bk	899	1,399	S	122+ 128GM		Y	Y	180	128	40	4	3	Y
PX-870	V		Bk/W/Wt	999	1,499	S	19	Y	Y	Y		256	40	4	3	Y
PX-S1000	S		Bk/Wt/Rd	649	949	S	18	Y	Y	Y		192	16	2	1 (3)	Y
PX-S3000	S	E	Bk	849	1,149	S	572+ 128GM	Y	Y	Y	200	192	16	2	1 (3)	Y
CDP-S350	S	E	Bk	549	849	S	572+ 128GM		Y		200	64	16	2	1 (3)	Y
CGP-700	V	E	Bk	849	1,149	S	422+ 128GM		Y		200	128	40	6	1 (3)	Y
AP-270	V		Bk/W/Wt	1,049	1,499	S	22		Y			192	16	2	3	Y
AP-470	V		Bk/W/Wt	1,499	1,899	S	22	Y	Y	Y		256	40	4	3	Y
AP-650	V	E	Bk	1,899	2,299	S	122+ 128GM	Y	Y	Y	180	256	60	4	3	Y
AP-710	V		Bk	2,499	2,999	S	26	Y	Y	Y		256	60	6	3	Y
GP-310	V		Bk/Wt	3,636	3,999	S	26	Y	Y	Y		256	100	6	3	Y
GP-510	V		BkP	4,909	5,999	S	35	Y	Y	Y		256	100	6	3	Y

Dexibell

Brand & Model	Form	Ensemble	Finish	Estimated Price	MSRP	Sound Source	Voices	Key Off	Sustain	String Resonance	Rhythms/Styles	Polyphony	Total Watts	Speakers	Piano Pedals	Half Pedal
VIVO P7	S	E	Bk	1,799	1,999	M/S	79	Y	Y	Y		UL	70	2	0 (2)	Y
VIVO S7 PRO	S	E	Wt	2,499	2,799	M/S	113	Y	Y	Y		UL		0	1 (3)	Y
VIVO S7 PRO M	S	E	Wt	2,999	3,499	M/S	113	Y	Y	Y		UL	70	2	1 (3)	Y
VIVO S9	S	E	Wt	3,999	4,499	M/S	185	Y	Y	Y		UL		0	1 (3)	Y
VIVO H1	S	E	Bk	2,634	2,799	M/S	79	Y	Y	Y		UL	70	2	3	Y
VIVO H3	V	E	Bk/Wt	2,899	2,899	M/S	79	Y	Y	Y		UL	70	4	3	Y
VIVO H7	V	E	Bk/Wt	3,999	3,999	M/S	79	Y	Y	Y		UL	112	5	3	Y
VIVO H7	V	E	Rd	4,199	4,199	M/S	79	Y	Y	Y		UL	112	5	3	Y
VIVO H7	V	E	EP/WtP/ RdP	4,499	4,499	M/S	79	Y	Y	Y		UL	112	5	3	Y

Dynatone

Brand & Model	Form	Ensemble	Finish	Estimated Price	MSRP	Sound Source	Voices	Key Off	Sustain	String Resonance	Rhythms/Styles	Polyphony	Total Watts	Speakers	Piano Pedals	Half Pedal
SDP-600	V		EP	3,809	5,795	S	33+ 128GM		Y	Y		256	100	4	3	Y
SDP-600	V		WtP	3,991	6,095	S	33+ 128GM		Y	Y		256	100	4	3	Y

Brand & Model	Action	Triple-Sensor Keys	Escapement	Wood Keys	Ivory Texture	Bluetooth	Vocal Support	Educational Features	External Storage	USB to Computer	USB Digital Audio	Recording Tracks	Warranty (Parts/Labor)	Dimensions WxDxH (Inches)	Weight (Pounds)

Casio *(continued)*

Brand & Model	Action	Triple-Sensor Keys	Escapement	Wood Keys	Ivory Texture	Bluetooth	Vocal Support	Educational Features	External Storage	USB to Computer	USB Digital Audio	Recording Tracks	Warranty (Parts/Labor)	Dimensions WxDxH (Inches)	Weight (Pounds)
PX-560	Weighted, Scaled, Hammer Action	Y			Y			Y	USB	Y	Y	17	3/3	52x12x6	27
PX-770	Weighted, Scaled, Hammer Action	Y			Y			Y		Y		12	3/3	55x12x31	69
PX-780	Weighted, Scaled, Hammer Action	Y			Y			Y	USB	Y	Y	17	3/3	53x12x33	70
PX-870	Weighted, Scaled, Hammer Action	Y			Y			Y	USB	Y	Y	2	3/3	55x12x30	76
PX-S1000	Weighted, Scaled, Hammer Action				Y	Y		Y	USB	Y		2	3/3	52x9x4	25
PX-S3000	Weighted, Scaled, Hammer Action				Y	Y		Y	USB	Y	Y	3	3/3	52x9x4	25
CDP-S350	Weighted, Scaled, Hammer Action				Y			Y	USB	Y		6	3/3	52x9x4	24
CGP-700	Weighted, Scaled, Hammer Action	Y			Y			Y	USB	Y	Y	16	3/3	52x12x31	57
AP-270	Weighted, Scaled, Hammer Action	Y		Y	Y			Y		Y		2	5/5	56x17x32	81
AP-470	Weighted, Scaled, Hammer Action	Y			Y			Y	USB	Y	Y	2	5/5	54x17x33	96
AP-650	Weighted, Scaled, Hammer Action	Y		Y	Y			Y	USB	Y	Y	17	5/5	54x17x36	111
AP-710	Weighted, Scaled, Hammer Action	Y			Y			Y	USB	Y	Y	2	5/5	54x17x36	106
GP-310	Weighted, Scaled, Hammer Action	Y	Y	Y				Y	USB	Y	Y	2	5/5	57x19x38	171
GP-510	Weighted, Scaled, Hammer Action	Y	Y	Y				Y	USB	Y	Y	2	5/5	57x19x38	171

Dexibell

Brand & Model	Action	Triple-Sensor Keys	Escapement	Wood Keys	Ivory Texture	Bluetooth	Vocal Support	Educational Features	External Storage	USB to Computer	USB Digital Audio	Recording Tracks	Warranty (Parts/Labor)	Dimensions WxDxH (Inches)	Weight (Pounds)
VIVO P7	Weighted	Y			Y			Y	USB	Y	Y	0	3	52x15x5	32
VIVO S7 PRO	Progressive Hammer	Y			Y	Y		Y	USB	Y	Y	0	3	50x14x5	39
VIVO S7 PRO M	Progressive Hammer	Y			Y			Y	USB	Y	Y	0	3	50x15x5	34
VIVO S9	Progressive Hammer	Y	Y	Y	Y			Y	USB	Y	Y	0	3	59x21x9	49
VIVO H1	Weighted	Y						Y	USB	Y	Y	0	5	56x14x31	99
VIVO H3	Weighted				Y			Y	USB	Y	Y	0	5	56x14x31	97
VIVO H7	Weighted, graded	Y			Y	Y		Y	USB	Y	Y	0	5	56x14x31	137
VIVO H7	Weighted, graded	Y			Y	Y		Y	USB	Y	Y	0	5	56x14x31	137
VIVO H7	Weighted, graded	Y			Y	Y		Y	USB	Y	Y	0	5	56x14x31	137

Dynatone

Brand & Model	Action	Triple-Sensor Keys	Escapement	Wood Keys	Ivory Texture	Bluetooth	Vocal Support	Educational Features	External Storage	USB to Computer	USB Digital Audio	Recording Tracks	Warranty (Parts/Labor)	Dimensions WxDxH (Inches)	Weight (Pounds)
SDP-600	New RHA-3W	Y	Y							Y	Y	1	3/3	55x16x39	218
SDP-600	New RHA-3W	Y	Y							Y	Y	1	3/3	55x16x39	218

Dynatone (continued)

Brand & Model	Form	Ensemble	Finish	Estimated Price	MSRP	Sound Source	Voices	Key Off	Sustain	String Resonance	Rhythms/Styles	Polyphony	Total Watts	Speakers	Piano Pedals	Half Pedal
SLP-210	V		R	1,627	2,195	S	18+ 128GM					81	24	2	3	
SLP-250H	V		Bk	2,173	3,095	S	33+ 128GM		Y	Y		256	30	4	3	Y
DPR-3200H	V	E	Bk	2,900	4,195	S	138	Y	Y	Y	80	256	100	4	3	Y
DPR-3500	V	E	Bk	3,445	5,095	S	138	Y	Y	Y	80	256	100	4	3	Y
SGP-600	G		EP	5,173	7,695	S	33+ 128GM		Y	Y		256	100	4	3	
SGP-600	G		WtP	5,355	7,995	S	33+ 128GM		Y	Y		256	100	4	3	
GPR-3500	G	E	EP	5,900	8,895	S	138	Y	Y	Y	80	256	100	6	3	
GPR-3500	G	E	WtP	6,082	9,195	S	138	Y	Y	Y	80	256	100	6	3	Y
VGP-4000Q	G	E	EP	9,173	14,495	S	138	Y	Y	Y	80	256	100	6	3	Y
VGP-4000Q	G	E	WtP	9,355	14,795	S	138	Y	Y	Y	80	256	100	6	3	Y

Galileo

Brand & Model	Form	Ensemble	Finish	Estimated Price	MSRP	Sound Source	Voices	Key Off	Sustain	String Resonance	Rhythms/Styles	Polyphony	Total Watts	Speakers	Piano Pedals	Half Pedal
YP200	V		R	2,495	3,495	S	19		Y	Y		128	80	4	3	
YP300	V		R	2,995	3,995	S	20		Y	Y		128	100	4	3	
YP300	V		EP	3,495	4,495	S	20		Y	Y		128	100	4	3	
Milano 3	V	E	R	4,995	5,995	S	138				100	64	40	4	3	
GYP300	G		EP/MP/WtP	6,995	8,995	S	20		Y	Y		128	120	4	3	
Milano 3G	G	E	EP	5,995	7,995	S	138				100	64	120	4	3	

Kawai

Brand & Model	Form	Ensemble	Finish	Estimated Price	MSRP	Sound Source	Voices	Key Off	Sustain	String Resonance	Rhythms/Styles	Polyphony	Total Watts	Speakers	Piano Pedals	Half Pedal
ES110	S		Bk/Wt	699	999	S	19	Y	Y	Y	100	192	14	2	1 (3)	Y
MP7SE	S		Bk	1,799	2,199	S	256	Y	Y	Y	100	256	0	0	1 (3)	Y
MP11SE	S		Bk	2,799	3,299	S	40	Y	Y	Y	100	256	0	0	3	Y
VPC1	S		Bk	1,849	2,149		0						0	0	3	Y
ES8	S		Bk/Wt	1,649	2,199	S	34	Y	Y	Y	100	256	30	2	1 (3)	Y
KDP70	V		R	899	1,099	S	15	Y		Y		192	16	2	3	Y
KDP110	V		R	1,199	1,549	S	15	Y		Y		192	40	2	3	Y
CN29	V		R/WtS/ES	1,959	2,399	S	19	Y	Y	Y	100	192	40	2	3	Y
CN39	V		R/WtS/ES	2,699	3,399	S	355	Y	Y	Y	100	256	40	4	3	Y
CA48	V		R	2,099	2,499	S	19	Y	Y	Y	100	192	40	4	3	Y

Dynatone (continued)

Brand & Model	Action	Triple-Sensor Keys	Escapement	Wood Keys	Ivory Texture	Bluetooth	Vocal Support	Educational Features	External Storage	USB to Computer	USB Digital Audio	Recording Tracks	Warranty (Parts/Labor)	Dimensions WxDxH (Inches)	Weight (Pounds)
SLP-210	New RHA						Y			Y	Y	2	3/3	54x16x33	75
SLP-250H	ARHA-I			Y			Y			Y	Y	1	3/3	54x16x33	95
DPR-3200H	ARHA-3I	Y		Y			Y		USB	Y	Y	2	3/3	55x19x35	127
DPR-3500	New RHA-3W	Y	Y			Y	Y		USB	Y	Y	2	3/3	55x19x35	119
SGP-600	New RHA-3W	Y	Y							Y	Y	1	3/3	55x36x31	176
SGP-600	New RHA-3W	Y	Y							Y	Y	1	3/3	55x36x31	176
GPR-3500	New RHA-3W	Y	Y			Y	Y		USB	Y	Y	2	3/3	56x46x36	209
GPR-3500	New RHA-3W	Y	Y			Y	Y		USB	Y	Y	2	3/3	56x46x36	209
VGP-4000Q	New RHA-3W	Y	Y			Y	Y		USB	Y	Y	2	3/3	60x56x40	440
VGP-4000Q	New RHA-3W	Y	Y			Y	Y		USB	Y	Y	2	3/3	60x56x40	440

Galileo

Brand & Model	Action	Triple-Sensor Keys	Escapement	Wood Keys	Ivory Texture	Bluetooth	Vocal Support	Educational Features	External Storage	USB to Computer	USB Digital Audio	Recording Tracks	Warranty (Parts/Labor)	Dimensions WxDxH (Inches)	Weight (Pounds)
YP200	Grand Response									Y		0	4/1	54x17x39	119
YP300	Graded Hammer									Y		3	4/1	54x20x41	137
YP300	Graded Hammer									Y		3	4/1	54x20x41	137
Milano 3	Graded Hammer									Y		3	4/1	56x20x34	154
GYP300	Graded Hammer									Y		3	4/1	56x29x35	209
Milano 3G	Graded Hammer									Y		3	4/1	56x29x35	200

Kawai

Brand & Model	Action	Triple-Sensor Keys	Escapement	Wood Keys	Ivory Texture	Bluetooth	Vocal Support	Educational Features	External Storage	USB to Computer	USB Digital Audio	Recording Tracks	Warranty (Parts/Labor)	Dimensions WxDxH (Inches)	Weight (Pounds)
ES110	RHC					Y	Y					1	3/3	52x11x6	26
MP7SE	RHIII	Y	Y	Y					USB	Y	Y	1	3/1	53x13x7	45
MP11SE	GF	Y	Y	Y	Y				USB	Y	Y	1	3/1	58x18x8	72
VPC1	RM3II	Y	Y	Y	Y					Y		0	3/1	54x18x8	65
ES8	RHIII	Y	Y		Y				USB	Y	Y	2	3/3	54x15x6	46
KDP70	RHC						Y			Y		1	3/3	54x16x34	77
KDP110	RHCII	Y				Y	Y			Y		1	3/3	54x16x34	86
CN29	RHIII	Y	Y		Y	Y	Y			Y		1	5/5	54x16x34	95
CN39	RHIII	Y	Y		Y	Y	Y		USB	Y		2	5/5	57x18x34	119
CA48	GFC	Y	Y	Y	Y	Y	Y			Y		1	5/5	53x18x35	126

Brand & Model	Form	Ensemble	Finish	Estimated Price	MSRP	Sound Source	Voices	Key Off	Sustain	String Resonance	Rhythms/Styles	Polyphony	Total Watts	Speakers	Piano Pedals	Half Pedal
Kawai (continued)																
CA48	V		ES	2,199	2,499	S	19	Y	Y	Y	100	192	40	4	3	Y
CA58	V		R	2,999	3,949	S	42	Y	Y	Y	100	256	100	4	3	Y
CA58	V		Wt/S/ES	3,099	3,999	S	42	Y	Y	Y	100	256	100	4	3	Y
CA79	V		R/Wt/S/ES	4,199	5,199	M/S	66	Y	Y	Y	100	256	100	6	3	Y
CA79	V		EP	4,799	5,899	M/S	66	Y	Y	Y	100	256	100	6	3	Y
CA99	V		R/Wt/S/ES	5,599	6,899	M/S	90	Y	Y	Y	100	256	135	6	3	Y
CA99	V		EP	6,399	7,899	M/S	90	Y	Y	Y	100	256	135	6	3	Y
NV5	V		EP	8,173	9,995	M/S	88	Y	Y	Y	100	256	135	6	3	Y
NV10	G		EP	12,445	15,999	M/S	88	Y	Y	Y	100	256	135	7	3	Y
Korg																
B2	S		Bk/Wt	500	720	S	12		Y	Y		120	30	2	1 (3)	Y
B2N	S		Bk	430	620	S	12		Y	Y		120	30	2	1 (3)	Y
SP280	S		Bk/Wt	800	1,230	S	30					120	44	2	1	
SV-2-88	S		Bk	2,000	2,900	S	72		Y	Y		128	0	0	1	Y
SV-2-88SP	S		Wt	2,200	3,200	S	72		Y	Y		128	30	2	1	Y
D1	S		Bk	670	930	S	30	Y	Y	Y		120	0	0	1	Y
XE20	V	E	Bk	800	1,200	S	705		Y		280	184	36	2	1 (3)	Y
B2SP	V		Bk/Wt	600	870	S	12		Y	Y		120	30	2	3	Y
LP180	V		Bk/Wt	650	930	S	10					120	22	2	3	Y
LP380	V		Bk/Wt	1,150	1,160	S	30					120	44	2	3	Y
G1 Air	V		Bk/Wt/R	1,800	1,950	S	32	Y	Y	Y		120	80	4	3	Y
C1 Air	V		Bk/Wt/R	1,450	1,600	S	30	Y	Y	Y		120	50	4	3	Y
Kurzweil																
MPS-110	S		Bk	999	1,299	S	152		Y		10	256	24	4	2	Y
MPS-120	S		Bk	1,299	1,699	S	152		Y		10	256	24	4	2	Y
KA-90	S	E	Bk	699	799	S	20		Y		50	128	60	4	1	
CUP-320	V		R	2,499	3,999	S	88	Y	Y	Y	69	128	50	4	3	Y

Kawai (continued)

Brand & Model	Action	Triple-Sensor Keys	Escapement	Wood Keys	Ivory Texture	Bluetooth	Vocal Support	Educational Features	External Storage	USB to Computer	USB Digital Audio	Recording Tracks	Warranty (Parts/Labor)	Dimensions WxDxH (Inches)	Weight (Pounds)
CA48	GFC	Y	Y	Y	Y	Y		Y			Y	1	5/5	53x18x35	126
CA58	GFC	Y	Y	Y	Y	Y		Y		USB	Y	2	5/5	57x18x36	161
CA58	GFC	Y	Y	Y	Y	Y		Y		USB	Y	2	5/5	57x18x36	161
CA79	GFIII	Y	Y	Y	Y	Y		Y		USB	Y	2	5/5	57x18x37	167
CA79	GFIII	Y	Y	Y	Y	Y		Y		USB	Y	2	5/5	57x18x37	174
CA99	GFIII	Y	Y	Y	Y	Y		Y		USB	Y	2	5/5	57x18x39	183
CA99	GFIII	Y	Y	Y	Y	Y		Y		USB	Y	2	5/5	57x18x39	196
NV5	Millennium III UP	Y	Y	Y	Y	Y		Y		USB	Y	2	5/5	59x18x43	249
NV10	Millennium III GP	Y	Y	Y	Y	Y		Y		USB	Y	2	5/5	58x25x36	279

Korg

Brand & Model	Action	Triple-Sensor Keys	Escapement	Wood Keys	Ivory Texture	Bluetooth	Vocal Support	Educational Features	External Storage	USB to Computer	USB Digital Audio	Recording Tracks	Warranty (Parts/Labor)	Dimensions WxDxH (Inches)	Weight (Pounds)
B2	NH							Y			Y	0	1/1	52x14x5	26
B2N	NH							Y			Y	0	1/1	52x14x5	21
SP280	NH											0	1/1	54x16x31	42
SV-2-88	RH3										Y	0	1/1	53x14x6	45
SV-2-88SP	RH3										Y	0	1/1	53x14x6	48
D1	RH3											0	1/1	53x11x5	36
XE20	NH										Y	12	1/1	52x14x5	26
B2SP	NH							Y			Y	0	1/1	52x14x30	47
LP180	NH										Y	0	1/1	54x11x31	51
LP380	RH3							Y				0	5/5	53x14x30	82
G1 Air	RH3					Y		Y			Y	2	5/5	53x15x33	91
C1 Air	RH3					Y		Y			Y	2	5/5	53x14x31	78

Kurzweil

Brand & Model	Action	Triple-Sensor Keys	Escapement	Wood Keys	Ivory Texture	Bluetooth	Vocal Support	Educational Features	External Storage	USB to Computer	USB Digital Audio	Recording Tracks	Warranty (Parts/Labor)	Dimensions WxDxH (Inches)	Weight (Pounds)
MPS-110	Weighted, graded	Y				Y				Y	Y	0	3/2	52x15x5	36
MPS-120	Weighted, graded	Y	Y	Y						Y	Y	0	3/2	52x15x5	38
KA-90	Weighted									Y		1	3/2	54x14x5	27
CUP-1	Weighted, graded					Y	Y			Y	Y	0	3/2	56x17x42	221

Brand & Model	Form	Ensemble	Finish	Estimated Price	MSRP	Sound Source	Voices	Key Off	Sustain	String Resonance	Rhythms/Styles	Polyphony	Total Watts	Speakers	Piano Pedals	Half Pedal
Kurzweil (continued)																
CUP-320	V		R	2,499	3,999	S	88	Y	Y	Y	69	128	50	4	3	Y
KAG-100	G	E	EP	2,499	3,999	S	200		Y		100	64	35	4	3	
MPG-100	G	E	EP	3,999	5,999	S	500		Y		200	128	60	4	3	Y
Nord																
Nord Piano 4	S		Rd	2,999	3,399	S	400		Y	Y		120	0	0	3	Y
Nord Grand	S		Rd/Bk	3,499	3,999	S	400		Y	Y		120	0	0	3	Y
Pearl River																
GP1100	G	E	PE/PWt/PRd	4,264	5,995	S	26	Y	Y	Y	30	512	85	4	3	Y
Physis																
H1	S		Al	2,995	4,995	M	192	Y	Y	Y		UL	0	0	3	Y
H2	S		Al	2,295	4,295	M	192	Y	Y	Y		UL	0	0	3	Y
K4EX	S		Bl	2,640	3,795	M	192	Y	Y	Y		UL	0	0	3	Y
V100	V		PE/PRd/PWt/SG/PBl	6,899	9,695	M	192	Y	Y	Y		UL	150	6	3	Y
G1000	G		EP			M	192	Y	Y	Y		UL	160	6	3	Y
Roland																
RD-2000	S		Bk	2,599	3,099	M/S	1100+	Y	Y	Y	200	UL/128	0	0	1 (3)	Y
V-Piano	S		Bk	6,999	7,999	M	24	Y	Y	Y		264	0	0	3	Y
GO:PIANO88	S		Bk	399	399	S	4		Y			128	20	2	1	
FP-10	S		Bk	499	649	M/S	15	Y	Y	Y		96	12	2	1	Y
FP-10C	V		Bk	589	779	M/S	15	Y	Y	Y		96	12	2	1	Y
FP-30	S	E	Bk/Wt	699	899	M/S	35	Y	Y	Y	8	128	22	2	1 (3)	Y
FP-30C	V	E	Bk/Wt	899	1,119	M/S	35	Y	Y	Y	8	128	22	2	3	Y
FP-60	S	E	Bk/Wt	1,499	1,799	M/S	355	Y	Y	Y	21	288	26	2	1 (3)	Y
FP-60C	V	E	Bk/Wt	1,849	2,299	M/S	355	Y	Y	Y	21	288	26	2	3	Y
FP-90	S	E	Bk/Wt	1,949	2,299	M	355	Y	Y	Y	21	UL/384	60	4	1 (3)	Y
FP-90C	V	E	Bk/Wt	2,349	2,799	M	355	Y	Y	Y	21	UL/384	60	4	3	Y

Brand & Model	Action	Triple-Sensor Keys	Escapement	Wood Keys	Ivory Texture	Bluetooth	Vocal Support	Educational Features	External Storage	USB to Computer	USB Digital Audio	Recording Tracks	Warranty (Parts/Labor)	Dimensions WxDxH (Inches)	Weight (Pounds)
Kurzweil *(continued)*															
CUP-320	Weighted, graded	Y		Y				Y		Y		1	3/2	56x19x35	105
KAG-100	Weighted				Y		Y		USB	Y	Y	2	3/2	56x30x35	150
MPG-100	Weighted, graded	Y						Y		Y		6	3/2	56x36x35	212
Nord															
Nord Piano 4	Fatar Weighted	Y								Y		0	1/1	51x13x5	40
Nord Grand	Kawai Weighted	Y		Y						Y		0	1/1	51x15x7	46
Pearl River															
GP1100	Fatar Weighted, Graded			Y			Y			Y		2	4/1	56x41x36	214
Physis															
H1	Tri-sensor, Hybrid	Y	Y	Y	Y				USB	Y	Y	16	3/1	54x13x4	58
H2	Lightweight Hammer, 3 sensors	Y	Y						USB	Y	Y	16	3/1	54x13x4	45
K4EX	Tri-sensor, Hybrid	Y	Y						USB	Y	Y	16	3/1	51x14x5	40
V100	Tri-sensor, Hybrid	Y	Y	Y	Y				USB	Y	Y	16	3/1	58x17x46	233
G1000	Tri-sensor, Hybrid	Y	Y	Y	Y				USB	Y		2	3/1	57x40x56	288
Roland															
RD-2000	PHA-50 Concert	Y	Y	Y	Y				USB	Y	Y	1	3/2	56x15x6	55
V-Piano	PHA III	Y	Y		Y				USB	Y	Y	0	3/2	56x21x7	84
GO:PIANO88	Touch Sensitive					Y		Y		Y			1/90	51x11x5	16
FP-10	PHA-4 Standard	Y	Y		Y	Y		Y		Y			3/2	51x11x6	27
FP-10C	PHA-4 Standard	Y	Y		Y	Y		Y		Y			3/2	51x13x36	44
FP-30	PHA-4 Standard	Y	Y		Y	Y		Y	USB	Y	Y	1	5/2	51x11x6	31
FP-30C	PHA-4 Standard	Y	Y		Y	Y		Y	USB	Y	Y	1	5/2	51x13x36	57
FP-60	PHA-4 Standard	Y			Y	Y		Y	USB	Y	Y	1	5/2	51x14x5	42
FP-60C	PHA-4 Standard	Y	Y		Y	Y		Y	USB	Y	Y	1	5/2	51x14x37	72
FP-90	PHA-50 Concert	Y	Y	Y	Y	Y	Y	Y	USB	Y	Y	2	5/2	53x15x5	52
FP-90C	PHA-50 Concert	Y	Y	Y	Y	Y	Y	Y	USB	Y	Y	2	5/2	53x15x37	83

Roland *(continued)*

Brand & Model	Form	Ensemble	Finish	Estimated Price	MSRP	Sound Source	Voices	Key Off	Sustain	String Resonance	Rhythms/Styles	Polyphony	Total Watts	Speakers	Piano Pedals	Half Pedal
DP-603	V	E	Bk	2,599	2,999	M	319	Y	Y	Y	21	UL/384	24	2	3	Y
DP-603	V	E	EP/WtP	3,099	3,499	M	319	Y	Y	Y	21	UL/384	24	2	3	Y
HP-504	V		R/ES	2,199	2,499	M/S	350	Y	Y	Y		128	24	2	3	Y
HP-601	V	E	R/ES/Wt	2,299	2,799	M/S	319	Y	Y	Y	21	288	28	2	3	Y
HP-603	V	E	R/ES/Wt	2,999	3,399	M	319	Y	Y	Y	21	UL/384	60	2	3	Y
HP-603A	V	E	R/ES/Wt	3,199	3,499	M	319	Y	Y	Y	21	UL/384	60	2	3	Y
HP-605	V	E	EP	4,349	4,999	M	319	Y	Y	Y	21	UL/384	74	6	3	Y
HP-605	V	E	R/ES/Wt	3,849	4,499	M	319	Y	Y	Y	21	UL/384	74	6	3	Y
HPi-50e	V	E	R	4,499	4,999	M/S	350	Y	Y	Y	50	128	74	4	3	Y
HP-702	V	E	O/R/ES/Wt	2,299	2,799	M	324	Y	Y	Y	21	UL/384	28	2	3	Y
HP-704	V	E	O/R/ES/Wt	3,199	3,499	M	324	Y	Y	Y	21	UL/384	60	4	3	Y
HP-704	V	E	EP	3,899	3,899	M	324	Y	Y	Y	21	UL/384	60	4	3	Y
LX-7	V	E	EP	5,999	6,899	M	319	Y	Y	Y	21	UL/384	74	6	3	Y
LX-7	V	E	W/ES	5,499	6,299	M	319	Y	Y	Y	21	UL/384	74	6	3	Y
LX-17	V	E	EP	6,499	7,599	M	319	Y	Y	Y	21	UL/384	74	8	3	Y
LX-17	V	E	WtP	6,799	7,999	M	319	Y	Y	Y	21	UL/384	74	8	3	Y
LX-705	V	E	O/R/ES	3,909	4,499	M	324	Y	Y	Y	21	UL/256	60	4	3	Y
LX-705	V	E	EP	4,764	4,899	M	324	Y	Y	Y	21	UL/256	60	4	3	Y
LX-706	V	E	R/ES	4,999	5,599	M	324	Y	Y	Y	21	UL/256	74	6	3	Y
LX-706	V	E	EP	6,299	6,299	M	324	Y	Y	Y	21	UL/256	74	6	3	Y
LX-708	V	E	ES	5,999	6,299	M	324	Y	Y	Y	21	UL/256	74	8	3	Y
LX-708	V	E	EP	7,199	7,199	M	324	Y	Y	Y	21	UL/256	74	8	3	Y
LX-708	V	E	WtP	7,499	7,499	M	324	Y	Y	Y	21	UL/256	74	8	3	Y
F-140R	V	E	ES/Wt	1,329	1,499	M/S	316	Y	Y	Y	72	128	24	2	3	Y
RP-102	V	E	Bk	899	1,199	M/S	318	Y	Y	Y	21	128	12	2	3	Y
RP-501R	V	E	Bk/Wt/R	1,599	1,999	M/S	316	Y	Y	Y	72	128	24	2	3	Y
GP-7 (V-Piano Grand)	G		EP	19,950	22,999	M	30	Y	Y	Y		264	240	8	3	Y
GP-607 (Mini Grand)	G	E	EP	7,545	7,599	M	319	Y	Y	Y	21	UL/384	70	5	3	Y
GP-607 (Mini Grand)	G	E	WtP	7,909	7,999	M	319	Y	Y	Y	21	UL/384	70	5	3	Y

Brand & Model	Action	Triple-Sensor Keys	Escapement	Wood Keys	Ivory Texture	Bluetooth	Vocal Support	Educational Features	External Storage	USB to Computer	USB Digital Audio	Recording Tracks	Warranty (Parts/Labor)	Dimensions WxDxH (Inches)	Weight (Pounds)
Roland (continued)															
DP-603	PHA-50 Concert	Y	Y	Y	Y	Y		Y	USB	Y	Y	3	5/2	55x14x31	104
DP-603	PHA-50 Concert	Y	Y	Y	Y	Y		Y	USB	Y	Y	3	5/2	55x14x31	104
HP-504	PHA4-Premium	Y	Y		Y			Y	USB	Y	Y	3	5/2	55x17x41	114
HP-601	PHA-50 Concert	Y	Y	Y	Y	Y		Y	USB	Y	Y	3	5/2	54x17x40	110
HP-603	PHA-50 Concert	Y	Y	Y	Y	Y		Y	USB	Y	Y	3	10/10	54x17x42	110
HP-603A	PHA-50 Concert	Y	Y	Y	Y	Y		Y	USB	Y	Y	3	10/10	54x17x42	110
HP-605	PHA-50 Concert	Y	Y	Y	Y	Y		Y	USB	Y	Y	3	10/10	54x17x44	119
HP-605	PHA-50 Concert	Y	Y	Y	Y	Y		Y	USB	Y	Y	3	10/10	54x17x44	119
HPi-50e	PHA4-Concert	Y	Y		Y			Y	USB	Y	Y	16	5/2	55x17x43	127
HP-702	PHA-4 Standard	Y	Y		Y	Y		Y	USB	Y	Y	3	5/2	54x18x42	120
HP-704	PHA-50 Concert	Y	Y	Y	Y	Y		Y	USB	Y	Y	3	10/10	54x19x44	131
HP-704	PHA-50 Concert	Y	Y	Y	Y	Y		Y	USB	Y	Y	3	10/10	54x19x44	134
LX-7	PHA-50 Concert	Y	Y	Y	Y	Y		Y	USB	Y	Y	3	10/10	55x18x41	170
LX-7	PHA-50 Concert	Y	Y	Y	Y	Y		Y	USB	Y	Y	3	10/10	55x18x41	170
LX-17	PHA-50 Concert	Y	Y	Y	Y	Y		Y	USB	Y	Y	3	10/10	55x19x42	193
LX-17	PHA-50 Concert	Y	Y	Y	Y	Y		Y		Y	Y	3	10/10	55x19x42	193
LX-705	PHA-50 Concert	Y	Y	Y	Y	Y		Y	USB	Y	Y	3	10/10	54x18x41	164
LX-705	PHA-50 Concert	Y	Y	Y	Y	Y		Y	USB	Y	Y	3	10/10	54x18x41	167
LX-706	PHA-100 Hybrid Grand	Y	Y	Y	Y	Y		Y	USB	Y	Y	3	10/10	54x19x44	212
LX-706	PHA-100 Hybrid Grand	Y	Y	Y	Y	Y		Y	USB	Y	Y	3	10/10	54x19x44	216
LX-708	PHA-100 Hybrid Grand	Y	Y	Y	Y	Y		Y	USB	Y	Y	3	10/10	55x19x46	240
LX-708	PHA-100 Hybrid Grand	Y	Y	Y	Y	Y		Y	USB	Y	Y	3	10/10	55x19x46	243
LX-708	PHA-100 Hybrid Grand	Y	Y	Y	Y	Y		Y	USB	Y	Y	3	10/10	55x19x46	243
F-140R	PHA-4-Standard	Y	Y		Y	Y		Y	USB	Y	Y	1	5/2	54x14x31	76
RP-102	PHA4-Standard	Y	Y		Y	Y		Y		Y		0	5/2	54x17x39	83
RP-501R	PHA-4 Standard	Y	Y		Y	Y		Y	USB	Y	Y	1	5/2	54x12x31	81
GP-7 (V-Piano Grand)	PHA III	Y	Y		Y				USB	Y	Y	1	5/2	59x59x61	375
GP-607 (Mini Grand)	PHA-50 Concert	Y	Y	Y	Y	Y		Y	USB	Y	Y	3	10/10	55x37x35	223
GP-607 (Mini Grand)	PHA-50 Concert	Y	Y	Y	Y	Y		Y	USB	Y	Y	3	10/10	55x37x35	223

Brand & Model	Form	Ensemble	Finish	Estimated Price	MSRP	Sound Source	Voices	Key Off	Sustain	String Resonance	Rhythms/Styles	Polyphony	Total Watts	Speakers	Piano Pedals	Half Pedal
Roland (continued)																
GP-609 (Grand Piano)	G	E	EP	10,999	10,999	M	319	Y	Y	Y	21	UL/384	74	7	3	Y
GP-609 (Grand Piano)	G	E	WtP	11,399	11,399	M	319	Y	Y	Y	21	UL/384	74	7	3	Y
Samick																
Ebony NEO	V		EP	4,089	4,095	S	10	Y	Y	Y			135	80	4	3	Y
SG-120	G	E	EP/WtP/RdP	3,907	4,295	S	377	Y	Y	Y		353	128	60	6	3	Y
SG-500	G	E	EP/WtP/RdP	4,816	5,295	S	377	Y	Y	Y		352	128	80	8	3	Y
Suzuki																
VG-88	V		R	1,599		S	16+ 128GM		Y	Y			189	40	4	3	
CTP-88	V	E	M	999	1,200	S	122+ 128GM		Y	Y	100	128	60	4	3	
MDG-300	G	E	EP	1,699	3,390	S	122+ 128GM		Y	Y	100	128	120	6	3	
MDG-330	G	E	EP	2,299	3,500	S	122+ 128GM		Y	Y	100	128	120	6	3	
MDG-400	G		EP	2,699	4,200	S	122+ 128GM		Y	Y	100	128	120	6	3	
MDG-4000ts	G		EP	3,399	5,899	S	672+ 256GM					240	128	250	6	3	
Williams																
Legato III	S		Bk	199	229	S	10	Y					64	40	2	1	
Allegro III	S		Bk	299	329	S	10	Y					64	60	2	1	
Rhapsody 2	V		WG/EP	499	900	S	12	Y					64	60	2	2	
Overture 2	V		EP/RdM	699	1,200	S	19+ 128GM	Y					64	60	4	3	
Symphony Grand	G	E	EP/RdM	1,499	1,999	S	46+ 128GM	Y	Y	Y	120	128	60	6	3	
Yamaha																
P45	S		Bk	500	599	S	10						64	12	2	1	Y
P121	S		Bk/Wt	600	899	M/S	24	Y					192		4		
P125	S		Bk/Wt	650	999	S	24				20	192	14	4	1 (3)	Y
P515	S		Bk/Wt	1,499	1,999	S	40+ 480XG	Y	Y	Y	40	256	40	4	1 (3)	Y
CP300	S		Bk	2,500	3,499	S	50+ 480XG	Y	Y	Y		128	60	2	3	Y

Roland *(continued)*

Brand & Model	Action	Triple-Sensor Keys	Escapement	Wood Keys	Ivory Texture	Bluetooth	Vocal Support	Educational Features	External Storage	USB to Computer	USB Digital Audio	Recording Tracks	Warranty (Parts/Labor)	Dimensions WxDxH (Inches)	Weight (Pounds)
GP-609 (Grand Piano)	PHA-50 Concert	Y	Y	Y	Y	Y		Y	USB	Y	Y	3	10/10	57x59x62	326
GP-609 (Grand Piano)	PHA-50 Concert	Y	Y	Y	Y	Y		Y	USB	Y	Y	3	10/10	57x59x62	326

Samick

Brand & Model	Action	Triple-Sensor Keys	Escapement	Wood Keys	Ivory Texture	Bluetooth	Vocal Support	Educational Features	External Storage	USB to Computer	USB Digital Audio	Recording Tracks	Warranty (Parts/Labor)	Dimensions WxDxH (Inches)	Weight (Pounds)
Ebony NEO	Graded	Y				Y	Y	Y	USB	Y	Y	2	3/3	57x19x41	170
SG-120	Graded	Y				Y	Y	Y	USB	Y	Y	5	3/3	56x35x29	170
SG-500	Graded	Y				Y	Y	Y	USB	Y	Y	5	3/3	56x49x35	290

Suzuki

Brand & Model	Action	Triple-Sensor Keys	Escapement	Wood Keys	Ivory Texture	Bluetooth	Vocal Support	Educational Features	External Storage	USB to Computer	USB Digital Audio	Recording Tracks	Warranty (Parts/Labor)	Dimensions WxDxH (Inches)	Weight (Pounds)
VG-88	Graded					Y	Y			Y		1	1/1	58x19x41	236
CTP-88	Graded						Y		SD	Y		3	1/1	54x20x40	175
MDG-300	Graded						Y		SD	Y		3	1/1	55x30x36	218
MDG-330	Graded						Y		SD	Y		3	1/1	57x39x36	330
MDG-400	Graded						Y		SD	Y		3	1/1	55x49x35	315
MDG-4000ts	Fatar Graded						Y		SD	Y		16	1/1	58x48x37	311

Williams

Brand & Model	Action	Triple-Sensor Keys	Escapement	Wood Keys	Ivory Texture	Bluetooth	Vocal Support	Educational Features	External Storage	USB to Computer	USB Digital Audio	Recording Tracks	Warranty (Parts/Labor)	Dimensions WxDxH (Inches)	Weight (Pounds)
Legato III	Semi-Weighted					Y		Y		Y		0	1/1	50x11x4	19
Allegro III	Weighted					Y		Y		Y		1	1/1	52x5x13	30
Rhapsody 2	Weighted							Y		Y		2	1/1	54x16x31	83
Overture 2	Weighted							Y	USB	Y		2	1/1	55x19x34	117
Symphony Grand	Graded, Weighted					Y		Y	USB	Y	Y	4	1/1	54x35x36	163

Yamaha

Brand & Model	Action	Triple-Sensor Keys	Escapement	Wood Keys	Ivory Texture	Bluetooth	Vocal Support	Educational Features	External Storage	USB to Computer	USB Digital Audio	Recording Tracks	Warranty (Parts/Labor)	Dimensions WxDxH (Inches)	Weight (Pounds)
P45	GHS									Y		0	3/3	52x12x6	26
P121	GHS									Y		0	3/3	44x12x7	22
P125	GHS									Y	Y	2	3/3	52x12x6	26
P515	NWX	Y	Y	Y	Y	Y			USB	Y	Y	16	3/3	53x14x7	48
CP300	GH									Y		16	3/3	54x18x7	72

Yamaha *(continued)*

Brand & Model	Form	Ensemble	Finish	Estimated Price	MSRP	Sound Source	Voices	Key Off	Sustain	String Resonance	Rhythms/Styles	Polyphony	Total Watts	Speakers	Piano Pedals	Half Pedal
CP40 Stage	S		Bk	1,400	2,399	M/S	297	Y	Y			128	0	0	1 (2)	Y
CP4 Stage	S		Bk	2,000	2,699	M/S	433	Y	Y			128	0	0	1 (2)	Y
CP1	S		Bk	5,000	5,999	M/S	17	Y	Y	Y		128	0	0	3	Y
YDP144	V		BkW/R	1,100	1,499	S	10					192	12	2	3	Y
YDPS34	V		BkW/R	1,100	1,399	S	10					192	12	2	3	Y
YDP164	V		BkW/R	1,500	1,999	S	10					192	40	4	3	Y
YDPS54	V		Bk/Wt	1,350	2,199	S	10					192	40	4	3	Y
YDP184	V		R	2,200	2,799	S	24	Y	Y	Y		256	60	2	3	Y
CSP150	V	E	Bk	3,500	3,999	S	721+ 480XG	Y	Y	Y	470	256	60	2	3	Y
CSP150	V	E	EP	4,000	4,599	S	721+ 480XG	Y	Y	Y	470	256	60	2	3	Y
CSP170	V	E	Bk	4,700	5,399	S	721+ 480XG	Y	Y	Y	470	256	180	4	3	Y
CSP170	V	E	EP	5,300	5,999	S	721+ 480XG	Y	Y	Y	470	256	180	4	3	Y
CLP625	V		EP	2,400	2,699	S	10	Y	Y	Y		256	40	2	3	Y
CLP625	V		Bk/R	2,000	2,299	S	10	Y	Y	Y		256	40	2	3	Y
CLP635	V		EP	3,200	3,599	S	36	Y	Y	Y	20	256	60	2	3	Y
CLP635	V		Bk/R/W	2,700	2,999	S	36	Y	Y	Y	20	256	60	2	3	Y
CLP645	V		EP	4,000	4,599	S	36	Y	Y	Y	20	256	100	4	3	Y
CLP645	V		Bk/R/W	3,500	3,999	S	36	Y	Y	Y	20	256	100	4	3	Y
CLP675	V		EP	5,300	5,999	S	36	Y	Y	Y	20	256	210	6	3	Y
CLP675	V		BK/R/W	4,700	5,199	S	36	Y	Y	Y	20	256	210	6	3	Y
CLP685	V		EP	6,600	7,499	S	49+ 480XG	Y	Y	Y	20	256	300	6	3	Y
CLP685	V		WtP	7,591	8,474	S	49+ 480XG	Y	Y	Y	20	256	300	6	3	Y
CLP685	V		Bk	5,800	6,499	S	49+ 480XG	Y	Y	Y	20	256	300	6	3	Y
CVP701	V	E	Bk	3,999	5,278	S	777+ 480XG	Y	Y	Y	310	256	50	2	3	Y
CVP701	V	E	EP	4,799	6,199	S	777+ 480XG	Y	Y	Y	310	256	50	2	3	Y
CVP805	V	E	Bk	7,400	9,199	S	1315+ 480XG	Y	Y	Y	525	256	130	4	3	Y
CVP805	V	E	EP	8,000	9,999	S	1315+ 480XG	Y	Y	Y	525	256	130	4	3	Y
CVP809	V	E	Bk	11,800	14,499	S	1605+ 480XG	Y	Y	Y	675	256	260	7	3	Y
CVP809	V	E	EP	12,500	14,999	S	1605+ 480XG	Y	Y	Y	675	256	260	7	3	Y

Yamaha *(continued)*

Brand & Model	Action	Triple-Sensor Keys	Escapement	Wood Keys	Ivory Texture	Bluetooth	Vocal Support	Educational Features	External Storage	USB to Computer	USB Digital Audio	Recording Tracks	Warranty (Parts/Labor)	Dimensions WxDxH (Inches)	Weight (Pounds)
CP40 Stage	GH								USB	Y	Y	0	3/3	52x14x6	36
CP4 Stage	NW-GH3	Y		Y	Y				USB	Y	Y	0	3/3	52x14x6	39
CP1	NW-Stage			Y	Y				USB	Y		0	3/3	55x17x7	60
YDP144	GHS									Y	Y	2	3/3	54x17x33	84
YDPS34	GHS									Y	Y	2	3/3	54x17x31	80
YDP164	GH3	Y			Y					Y	Y	2	3/3	54x17x34	93
YDPS54	GH3	Y			Y					Y	Y	2	3/3	55x12x31	80
YDP184	GH3	Y			Y				USB	Y		16	3/3	57x36x18	123
CSP150	GH3X	Y	Y		Y		Y	Y	USB-Tablet	Y	Y	16	5/5	56x18x40	127
CSP150	GH3X	Y	Y		Y		Y	Y	USB-Tablet	Y	Y	17	5/6	56x18x40	127
CSP170	NWX	Y	Y	Y	Y		Y	Y	USB-Tablet	Y	Y	18	5/7	56x18x40	147
CSP170	NWX	Y	Y	Y	Y		Y	Y	USB-Tablet	Y	Y	19	5/8	56x18x40	147
CLP625	GH3X	Y	Y		Y					Y		2	5/5	53x16x33	95
CLP625	GH3X	Y	Y		Y					Y		2	5/5	53x16x33	99
CLP635	GH3X	Y	Y		Y			Y	USB	Y	Y	16	5/5	58x18x37	123
CLP635	GH3X	Y	Y		Y			Y	USB	Y	Y	16	5/5	58x18x37	137
CLP645	NWX	Y	Y	Y	Y	Y		Y	USB	Y	Y	16	5/5	58x18x37	132
CLP645	NWX	Y	Y	Y	Y	Y		Y	USB	Y	Y	16	5/5	58x18x37	146
CLP675	GrandTouch	Y	Y	Y	Y	Y		Y	USB	Y	Y	16	5/5	58x19x38	152
CLP675	GrandTouch	Y	Y	Y	Y	Y		Y	USB	Y	Y	16	5/5	58x19x38	157
CLP685	GrandTouch	Y	Y	Y	Y	Y		Y	USB	Y	Y	16	5/5	58x19x41	183
CLP685	GrandTouch	Y	Y	Y	Y	Y		Y	USB	Y	Y	16	5/5	58x19x41	183
CLP685	GrandTouch	Y	Y	Y	Y	Y		Y	USB	Y	Y	16	5/5	58x19x41	196
CVP701	GH3X		Y		Y		Y	Y	USB	Y		16	5/5	53x24x36	130
CVP701	GH3X	Y	Y		Y		Y	Y	USB	Y		16	5/5	53x24x36	130
CVP805	GrandTouch		Y		Y	Y	Y	Y	USB	Y		16	5/5	56x24x41	185
CVP805	GrandTouch		Y		Y	Y	Y	Y	USB	Y		16	5/5	56x24x41	185
CVP809	GrandTouch		Y		Y	Y	Y	Y	USB	Y		16	5/5	56x24x41	185
CVP809	GrandTouch		Y		Y	Y	Y	Y	USB	Y		16	5/5	56x24x41	185

Yamaha *(continued)*

Brand & Model	Form	Ensemble	Finish	Estimated Price	MSRP	Sound Source	Voices	Key Off	Sustain	String Resonance	Rhythms/Styles	Polyphony	Total Watts	Speakers	Piano Pedals	Half Pedal
CVP809	V	E	WtP	13,000	15,999	S	1605+480XG	Y	Y	Y	675	256	260	7	3	Y
NU1X	V		EP	6,362	7,699	S	15	Y	Y	Y		256	180	4	3	Y
NU1X	V		WtP	6,907	7,899	S	15	Y	Y	Y		256	180	4	3	Y
N1X	G		EP	9,725	10,999	S	15	Y	Y	Y		256	180	6	3	Y
N2	G		EP	12,635	14,999	S	5	Y	Y	Y		256	500	12	3	Y
N3X	G		EP	18,816	22,199	S	10	Y	Y	Y		256	500	12	3	Y
CLP665GP	G		EP	5,500	6,199	S	36	Y	Y	Y	20	256	70	4	3	Y
CLP665GP	G		WtP	6,300	6,999	S	36	Y	Y	Y	20	256	70	4	3	Y
CLP695GP	G	E	WtP	8,500	9,999	S	49+480XG	Y	Y	Y	20	256	300	6	3	Y
CLP695GP	G	E	EP	7,500	8,499	S	49+480XG	Y	Y	Y	20	256	300	6	3	Y
CVP809GP	G	E	EP	16,000	19,999	S	1605+480XG	Y	Y	Y	675	256	260	6	3	Y
CVP809GP	G	E	WtP	17,000	21,999	S	1605+480XG	Y	Y	Y	675	256	260	6	3	Y

Yamaha *(continued)*

Brand & Model	Action	Triple-Sensor Keys	Escapement	Wood Keys	Ivory Texture	Bluetooth	Vocal Support	Educational Features	External Storage	USB to Computer	USB Digital Audio	Recording Tracks	Warranty (Parts/Labor)	Dimensions WxDxH (Inches)	Weight (Pounds)
CVP809	GrandTouch	Y	Y	Y	Y	Y		Y	USB	Y		16	5/5	56x24x41	185
NU1X	Specialized Upright		Y		Y				USB	Y	Y	1	5/5	60x18x40	240
NU1X	Specialized Upright		Y		Y				USB	Y	Y	1	5/5	60x18x40	240
N1X	Specialized Grand	Y	Y		Y				USB	Y	Y	1	5/5	58x24x39	257
N2	Specialized Grand	Y	Y	Y					USB			1	5/5	58x21x40	313
N3X	Specialized Grand	Y	Y	Y					USB	Y	Y	1	5/5	58x47x40	439
CLP665GP	GH3X	Y	Y		Y	Y		Y	USB	Y	Y	16	1	56x45x37	227
CLP665GP	GH3X	Y	Y		Y	Y		Y	USB	Y	Y	16	1	56x45x37	227
CLP695GP	GH3X	Y	Y	Y	Y	Y		Y	USB	Y	Y	16	1	56x4836	280
CLP695GP	GH3X	Y	Y	Y	Y	Y		Y	USB	Y	Y	16	1	56x4836	280
CVP809GP	GrandTouch	Y	Y	Y	Y	Y	Y	Y	USB	Y	Y	16	5/5	56x48x42	275
CVP809GP	GrandTouch	Y	Y	Y	Y	Y	Y	Y	USB	Y	Y	16	5/5	56x48x42	275